JANE EYRE

Charlotte Brontë

SPARKNOTES

Contributors: Brian Phillips, Katie Mannheimer, Sarah Friedberg, John Crowther

Note: This SparkNote uses the Bantam Classic edition of *Jane Eyre*. Some editions divide the novel into three volumes. In these editions, Volume One covers Chapters 1–15, Volume Two covers Chapters 16–26, and Volume Three covers Chapters 27–38.

This edition published by Spark Publishing

Spark Publishing
A Division of SparkNotes LLC
76 9th Avenue, 11th Floor
New York, NY 10011

ISBN 1-58663-364-3

Text design by Rhea Braunstein
Text composition by Jackson Typesetting

Printed and bound in the United States of America

01 02 03 04 05 SN 9 8 7 6 5 4 3 2 1

RRD-C

http://www.sparknotes.com

STOPPING TO BUY SPARKNOTES ON A SNOWY EVENING

Whose words these are you *think* you know.
Your paper's due tomorrow, though;
We're glad to see you stopping here
To get some help before you go.

Lost your course? You'll find it here.
Face tests and essays without fear.
Between the words, good grades at stake:
Get great results throughout the year.

Once school bells caused your heart to quake
As teachers circled each mistake.
Use SparkNotes and no longer weep,
Ace every single test you take.

Yes, books are lovely, dark, and deep,
But only what you grasp you keep,
With hours to go before you sleep,
With hours to go before you sleep.

CONTENTS

Charlotte Brontë was born in Yorkshire, England on April 21, 1816 to Maria Branwell and Patrick Brontë. Because Charlotte's mother died when Charlotte was five years old, Charlotte's aunt, a devout Methodist, helped her brother-in-law raise his children. In 1824 Charlotte and three of her sisters—Maria, Elizabeth, and Emily—were sent to Cowan Bridge, a school for clergymen's daughters. When an outbreak of tuberculosis killed Maria and Elizabeth, Charlotte and Emily were brought home. Several years later, Charlotte returned to school, this time in Roe Head, England. She became a teacher at the school in 1835 but decided after several years to become a private governess instead. She was hired to live with and tutor the children of the wealthy Sidgewick family in 1839, but the job was a misery to her and she soon left it. Once Charlotte recognized that her dream of starting her own school was not immediately realizable, however, she returned to working as a governess, this time for a different family. Finding herself equally disappointed with governess work the second time around, Charlotte recruited her sisters to join her in more serious preparation for the establishment of a school.

Although the Brontës' school was unsuccessful, their literary projects flourished. At a young age, the children created a fictional world they named Angria, and their many stories, poems, and plays were early predictors of shared writing talent that eventually led Emily, Anne, and Charlotte to careers as novelists. As adults, Charlotte suggested that she, Anne, and Emily collaborate on a book of poems. The three sisters published under male pseudonyms: Charlotte's was Currer Bell, while Emily and Anne wrote as Ellis and Acton Bell, respectively. When the poetry volume received little public notice, the sisters decided to work on separate novels but retained the same pseudonyms. Anne and Emily produced their masterpieces in 1847, but Charlotte's first book, *The Professor,* never found a willing publisher during her lifetime. Charlotte wrote *Jane Eyre* later that year. The book, a critique of Victorian assumptions about gender and social class, became one of the most successful novels of its era, both critically and commercially.

Autobiographical elements are recognizable throughout *Jane Eyre*. Jane's experience at Lowood School, where her dearest friend dies of tuberculosis, recalls the death of Charlotte's sisters at Cowan Bridge. The hypocritical religious fervor of the headmaster, Mr. Brocklehurst, is based in part on that of the Reverend Carus Wilson, the Evangelical minister who ran Cowan Bridge. Charlotte took revenge upon the school that treated her so poorly by using it as the basis for the fictional Lowood. Jane's friend Helen Burns's tragic death from tuberculosis recalls the deaths of two of Charlotte's sisters, Maria and Elizabeth, who succumbed to the same disease during their time at Cowan Bridge. Additionally, John Reed's decline into alcoholism and dissolution is most likely modeled upon the life of Charlotte Brontë's brother Branwell, who slid into opium and alcohol addictions in the years preceding his death. Finally, like Charlotte, Jane becomes a governess—a comparatively neutral vantage point from which to observe and describe the oppressive social ideas and practices of nineteenth-century Victorian society.

The plot of *Jane Eyre* follows the form of a *Bildungsroman,* which is a novel that tells the story of a child's maturation and focuses on the emotions and experiences that accompany and incite his or her growth to adulthood. In *Jane Eyre,* there are five distinct stages of development, each linked to a particular place: Jane's childhood at Gateshead, her education at the Lowood School, her time as Adele's governess at Thornfield, her time with the Rivers family at Morton and at Marsh End (also called Moor House), and her reunion with and marriage to Rochester at Ferndean. From these various experiences, Jane becomes the mature and steady-handed woman who narrates the novel retrospectively.

But the *Bildungsroman* plot of *Jane Eyre,* and the book's element of social criticism, are filtered through a third literary tradition—that of the Gothic horror story. Like the *Bildungsroman,* the Gothic genre originated in Germany. It became popular in England in the late eighteenth century, and it generally describes supernatural experiences, remote landscapes, and mysterious occurrences, all of which are intended to create an atmosphere of suspense and fear. Jane's encounters with ghosts, dark secrets, and sinister plots add a potent and lingering sense of fantasy and mystery to the novel.

After the success of *Jane Eyre,* Charlotte revealed her identity to her publisher and went on to write several other novels, most notably *Shirley* in 1849. In the years that followed, she became a respected member of London's literary set. But the deaths of siblings Emily and Branwell in 1848, and of Anne in 1849, left her feeling dejected and emotionally isolated. In 1854, she wed the Reverend Arthur Nicholls, despite the fact that she did not love him. She died of pneumonia, while pregnant, the following year.

J ane Eyre is a young orphan being raised by Mrs. Reed, her cruel, wealthy aunt. A servant named Bessie provides Jane with some of the few kindnesses she receives, telling her stories and singing songs to her. One day, as punishment for fighting with her bullying cousin John Reed, Jane's aunt imprisons Jane in the red-room, the room in which Jane's Uncle Reed died. While locked in, Jane, believing that she sees her uncle's ghost, screams and faints. She wakes to find herself in the care of Bessie and the kindly apothecary Mr. Lloyd, who suggests to Mrs. Reed that Jane be sent away to school. To Jane's delight, Mrs. Reed concurs.

Once at the Lowood School, Jane finds that her life is far from idyllic. The school's headmaster is Mr. Brocklehurst, a cruel, hypocritical, and abusive man. Brocklehurst preaches a doctrine of poverty and privation to his students while using the school's funds to provide a wealthy and opulent lifestyle for his own family. At Lowood, Jane befriends a young girl named Helen Burns, whose strong, martyrlike attitude toward the school's miseries is both helpful and displeasing to Jane. A massive typhus epidemic sweeps Lowood, and Helen dies of consumption. The epidemic also results in the departure of Mr. Brocklehurst by attracting attention to the insalubrious conditions at Lowood. After a group of more sympathetic gentlemen takes Brocklehurst's place, Jane's life improves dramatically. She spends eight more years at Lowood, six as a student and two as a teacher.

After teaching for two years, Jane yearns for new experiences. She accepts a governess position at a manor called Thornfield, where she teaches a lively French girl named Adèle. The distinguished housekeeper Mrs. Fairfax presides over the estate. Jane's employer at Thornfield is a dark, impassioned man named Rochester, with whom Jane finds herself falling secretly in love. She saves Rochester from a fire one night, which he claims was started by a drunken servant named Grace Poole. But because Grace Poole continues to work at Thornfield, Jane concludes that she has not been told the entire story. Jane sinks into despondency when

Rochester brings home a beautiful but vicious woman named Blanche Ingram. Jane expects Rochester to propose to Blanche. But Rochester instead proposes to Jane, who accepts almost disbelievingly.

The wedding day arrives, and as Jane and Mr. Rochester prepare to exchange their vows, the voice of Mr. Mason cries out that Rochester already has a wife. Mason introduces himself as the brother of that wife—a woman named Bertha. Mr. Mason testifies that Bertha, whom Rochester married when he was a young man in Jamaica, is still alive. Rochester does not deny Mason's claims, but he explains that Bertha has gone mad. He takes the wedding party back to Thornfield, where they witness the insane Bertha Mason scurrying around on all fours and growling like an animal. Rochester keeps Bertha hidden on the third story of Thornfield and pays Grace Poole to keep his wife under control. Bertha was the real cause of the mysterious fire earlier in the story. Knowing that it is impossible for her to be with Rochester, Jane flees Thornfield.

Penniless and hungry, Jane is forced to sleep outdoors and beg for food. At last, three siblings who live in a manor alternatively called Marsh End and Moor House take her in. Their names are Mary, Diana, and St. John (pronounced "Sinjin") Rivers, and Jane quickly becomes friends with them. St. John is a clergyman, and he finds Jane a job teaching at a charity school in Morton. He surprises her one day by declaring that her uncle, John Eyre, has died and left her a large fortune: 20,000 pounds. When Jane asks how he received this news, he shocks her further by declaring that her uncle was also his uncle: Jane and the Riverses are cousins. Jane immediately decides to share her inheritance equally with her three newfound relatives.

St. John decides to travel to India as a missionary, and he urges Jane to accompany him—as his wife. Jane agrees to go to India but refuses to marry her cousin because she does not love him. St. John pressures her to reconsider, and she nearly gives in. However, she realizes that she cannot abandon forever the man she truly loves when one night she hears Rochester's voice calling her name over the moors. Jane immediately hurries back to Thornfield and finds that it has been burned to the ground by Bertha Mason, who lost her life in the fire. Rochester saved the servants but lost his eyesight and one of his hands. Jane travels on to Rochester's new residence, Ferndean, where he lives with two servants named John and Mary.

At Ferndean, Rochester and Jane rebuild their relationship and soon marry. At the end of her story, Jane writes that she has been married for ten blissful years and that she and Rochester enjoy perfect equality in their life together. She says that after two years of blindness, Rochester regained sight in one eye and was able to behold their first son at his birth.

Jane Eyre—The protagonist and narrator of the novel, Jane is an intelligent, honest, plain-featured young girl forced to contend with oppression, inequality, and hardship. Although she meets with a series of individuals who threaten her autonomy, Jane repeatedly succeeds at asserting herself and maintains her principles of justice, human dignity, and morality. She also values intellectual and emotional fulfillment. Her strong belief in gender and social equality challenges the Victorian prejudices against women and the poor.

Edward Rochester—Jane's employer and the master of Thornfield, Rochester is a wealthy, passionate man with a dark secret that provides much of the novel's suspense. Rochester is unconventional, ready to set aside polite manners, propriety, and consideration of social class in order to interact with Jane frankly and directly. He is rash and impetuous and has spent much of his adult life roaming about Europe in an attempt to avoid the consequences of his youthful indiscretions. His problems are partly the result of his own recklessness, but he is a sympathetic figure because he has suffered for so long as a result of his early marriage to Bertha.

St. John Rivers—Along with his sisters, Mary and Diana, St. John (pronounced "Sinjin") serves as Jane's benefactor after she runs away from Thornfield, giving her food and shelter. The minister at Morton, St. John is cold, reserved, and often controlling in his interactions with others. Because he is entirely alienated from his feelings and devoted solely to an austere ambition, St. John serves as a foil to Edward Rochester.

Mrs. Reed—Mrs. Reed is Jane's cruel aunt, who raises her at Gateshead Hall until Jane is sent away to school at age ten. Later in her life, Jane attempts reconciliation with her aunt, but the old woman continues to resent her because her husband had always loved Jane more than his own children.

Bessie Lee—The maid at Gateshead, Bessie is the only figure in Jane's childhood who regularly treats her kindly, telling her stories and singing her songs. Bessie later marries Robert Leaven, the Reeds' coachman.

Mr. Lloyd—Mr. Lloyd is the Reeds' apothecary, who suggests that Jane be sent away to school. Always kind to Jane, Mr. Lloyd writes a letter to Miss Temple confirming Jane's story about her childhood and clearing Jane of Mrs. Reed's charge that she is a liar.

Georgiana Reed—Georgiana Reed is Jane's cousin and one of Mrs. Reed's two daughters. The beautiful Georgiana treats Jane cruelly when they are children, but later in their lives she befriends her cousin and confides in her. Georgiana attempts to elope with a man named Lord Edwin Vere, but her sister, Eliza, alerts Mrs. Reed of the arrangement and sabotages the plan. After Mrs. Reed dies, Georgiana marries a wealthy man.

Eliza Reed—Eliza Reed is Jane's cousin and one of Mrs. Reed's two daughters (along with her sister, Georgiana). Not as beautiful as her sister, Eliza devotes herself somewhat self-righteously to the church and eventually goes to a convent in France where she becomes the Mother Superior.

John Reed—John Reed is Jane's cousin, Mrs. Reed's son, and brother to Eliza and Georgiana. John treats Jane with appalling cruelty during their childhood and later falls into a life of drinking and gambling. John commits suicide midway through the novel when his mother ceases to pay his debts for him.

Helen Burns—Helen Burns is Jane's close friend at the Lowood School. She endures her miserable life there with a passive dignity that Jane cannot understand. Helen dies of consumption in Jane's arms.

Mr. Brocklehurst—The cruel, hypocritical master of the Lowood School, Mr. Brocklehurst preaches a doctrine of privation, while stealing from the school to support his luxurious lifestyle. After a typhus epidemic sweeps Lowood, Brocklehurst's shifty and dishonest practices are brought to light and he is publicly discredited.

Maria Temple—Maria Temple is a kind teacher at Lowood, who treats Jane and Helen with respect and compassion. Along with Bessie Lee, she serves as one of Jane's first positive female role models. Miss Temple helps clear Jane of Mrs. Reed's accusations against her.

Miss Scatcherd—Jane's sour and vicious teacher at Lowood, Miss Scatcherd behaves with particular cruelty toward Helen.

Alice Fairfax—Alice Fairfax is the housekeeper at Thornfield Hall. She is the first to tell Jane that the mysterious laughter often heard echoing through the halls is, in fact, the laughter of Grace Poole—a lie that Rochester himself often repeats.

Bertha Mason—Rochester's clandestine wife, Bertha Mason is a formerly beautiful and wealthy Creole woman who has become insane, violent, and bestial. She lives locked in a secret room on the third story of Thornfield and is guarded by Grace Poole, whose occasional bouts of inebriation sometimes enable Bertha to escape. Bertha eventually burns down Thornfield, plunging to her death in the flames.

Grace Poole—Grace Poole is Bertha Mason's keeper at Thornfield, whose drunken carelessness frequently allows Bertha to escape. When Jane first arrives at Thornfield, Mrs. Fairfax attributes to Grace all evidence of Bertha's misdeeds.

Adèle Varens—Jane's pupil at Thornfield, Adèle Varens is a lively though somewhat spoiled child from France. Rochester brought her to Thornfield after her mother, Celine, abandoned her. Although Celine was once Rochester's mistress, he does not believe himself to be Adèle's father.

Celine Varens—Celine Varens is a French opera dancer with whom Rochester once had an affair. Although Rochester does not believe Celine's claims that he fathered her daughter Adèle, he nonetheless brought the girl to England when Celine abandoned her. Rochester had broken off his relationship with Celine after learning that Celine was unfaithful to him and interested only in his money.

Sophie—Sophie is Adèle's French nurse at Thornfield.

Richard Mason—Richard Mason is Bertha's brother. During a visit to Thornfield, he is injured by his mad sister. After learning of Rochester's intent to marry Jane, Mason arrives with the solicitor Briggs in order to thwart the wedding and reveal the truth of Rochester's prior marriage.

Mr. Briggs—John Eyre's attorney, Mr. Briggs helps Richard Mason prevent Jane's wedding to Rochester when he learns of the existence of Bertha Mason, Rochester's wife. After John Eyre's death, Briggs searches for Jane in order to give her her inheritance.

Blanche Ingram—Blanche Ingram is a beautiful socialite who despises Jane and hopes to marry Rochester for his money.

Diana Rivers—Diana Rivers is Jane's cousin, and the sister of St. John and Mary. Diana is a kind and intelligent person, and she urges Jane not to go to India with St. John. She serves as a model for Jane of an intellectually gifted and independent woman.

Mary Rivers—Mary Rivers is Jane's cousin, the sister of St. John and Diana. Mary is a kind and intelligent young woman who is forced to work as a governess after her father loses his fortune. Like her sister, she serves as a model for Jane of an independent woman who is also able to maintain close relationships with others and a sense of meaning in her life.

Rosamond Oliver—Rosamond is the beautiful daughter of Mr. Oliver, Morton's wealthiest inhabitant. Rosamond gives money to the school in Morton where Jane works. Although she is in love with St. John, she becomes engaged to the wealthy Mr. Granby.

John Eyre—John Eyre is Jane's uncle, who leaves her his vast fortune of 20,000 pounds.

Uncle Reed—Uncle Reed is Mrs. Reed's late husband. In her childhood, Jane believes that she feels the presence of his ghost. Because he was always fond of Jane and her mother (his sister), Uncle Reed made his wife promise that she would raise Jane as her own child. It is a promise that Mrs. Reed does not keep.

JANE EYRE

The development of Jane Eyre's character is central to the novel. From the beginning, Jane possesses a sense of her self-worth and dignity, a commitment to justice and principle, a trust in God, and a passionate disposition. Her integrity is continually tested over the course of the novel, and Jane must learn to balance the frequently conflicting aspects of herself so as to find contentment.

An orphan since early childhood, Jane feels exiled and ostracized at the beginning of the novel, and the cruel treatment she receives from her Aunt Reed and her cousins only exacerbates her feeling of alienation. Afraid that she will never find a true sense of home or community, Jane feels the need to belong somewhere, to find "kin," or at least "kindred spirits." This desire tempers her equally intense need for autonomy and freedom.

In her search for freedom, Jane also struggles with the question of what *type* of freedom she wants. While Rochester initially offers Jane a chance to liberate her passions, Jane comes to realize that such freedom could also mean enslavement—by living as Rochester's mistress, she would be sacrificing her dignity and integrity for the sake of her feelings. St. John Rivers offers Jane another kind of freedom: the freedom to act unreservedly on her principles. He opens to Jane the possibility of exercising her talents fully by working and living with him in India. Jane eventually realizes, though, that this freedom would also constitute a form of imprisonment, because she would be forced to keep her true feelings and her true passions always in check.

Charlotte Brontë may have created the character of Jane Eyre as a means of coming to terms with elements of her own life. Much evidence suggests that Brontë, too, struggled to find a balance between love and freedom and to find others who understood her. At many points in the book, Jane voices the author's then-radical opinions on religion, social class, and gender.

EDWARD ROCHESTER

Despite his stern manner and not particularly handsome appearance, Edward Rochester wins Jane's heart, because she feels they are kindred spirits, and because he is the first person in the novel to offer Jane lasting love and a real home. Although Rochester is Jane's social and economic superior, and although men were widely considered to be naturally superior to women in the Victorian period, Jane is Rochester's intellectual equal. Moreover, after their marriage is interrupted by the disclosure that Rochester is already married to Bertha Mason, Jane is proven to be Rochester's moral superior.

Rochester regrets his former libertinism and lustfulness; nevertheless, he has proven himself to be weaker in many ways than Jane. Jane feels that living with Rochester as his mistress would mean the loss of her dignity. Ultimately, she would become degraded and dependent upon Rochester for love, while unprotected by any true marriage bond. Jane will only enter into marriage with Rochester after she has gained a fortune and a family, and after she has been on the verge of abandoning passion altogether. She waits until she is not unduly influenced by her own poverty, loneliness, psychological vulnerability, or passion. Additionally, because Rochester has been blinded by the fire and has lost his manor house at the end of the novel, he has become weaker while Jane has grown in strength—Jane claims that they are equals, but the marriage dynamic has actually tipped in her favor.

ST. JOHN RIVERS

St. John Rivers is a foil to Edward Rochester. Whereas Rochester is passionate, St. John is austere and ambitious. Jane often describes Rochester's eyes as flashing and flaming, whereas she constantly associates St. John with rock, ice, and snow. Marriage with Rochester represents the abandonment of principle for the consummation of passion, but marriage to St. John would mean sacrificing passion for principle. When he invites her to come to India with him as a missionary, St. John offers Jane the chance to make a more meaningful contribution to society than she would as a housewife. At the same time, life with St. John would mean life without true love, in which Jane's need for spiritual solace would be filled only by retreat into the recesses of her own soul. Independence would be accompanied by loneliness, and joining St. John would require Jane to neglect her own legitimate needs for love and emotional support. Her consideration of St. John's proposal leads Jane to understand that, paradoxically, a large part of one's personal freedom is found in a relationship of mutual emotional dependence.

HELEN BURNS

Helen Burns, Jane's friend at Lowood School, serves as a foil to Mr. Brocklehurst as well as to Jane. While Mr. Brocklehurst embodies an evangelical form of religion that seeks to strip others of their excessive pride or of their ability to take pleasure in worldly things, Helen represents a mode of Christianity that stresses tolerance and acceptance. Brocklehurst uses religion to gain power and to control others; Helen ascetically trusts her own faith and turns the other cheek to Lowood's harsh policies.

Although Helen manifests a certain strength and intellectual maturity, her efforts involve self-negation rather than self-assertion, and Helen's submissive and ascetic nature highlights Jane's more headstrong character. Like Jane, Helen is an orphan who longs for a home, but Helen believes that she will find this home in Heaven rather than Northern England. And while Helen is not oblivious to the injustices the girls suffer at Lowood, she believes that justice will be found in God's ultimate judgment—God will reward the good and punish the evil. Jane, on the other hand, is unable to have such blind faith. Her quest is for love and happiness in *this* world. Nevertheless, she counts on God for support and guidance in her search.

THEMES

Themes are the fundamental and often universal ideas explored in a literary work.

Love versus Autonomy

Jane Eyre is very much the story of a quest to be loved. Jane searches, not just for romantic love, but also for a sense of being valued, of belonging. Thus Jane says to Helen Burns: "to gain some real affection from you, or Miss Temple, or any other whom I truly love, I would willingly submit to have the bone of my arm broken, or to let a bull toss me, or to stand behind a kicking horse, and let it dash its hoof at my chest" (Chapter 8). Yet, over the course of the book, Jane must learn how to gain love *without* sacrificing and harming herself in the process.

Her fear of losing her autonomy motivates her refusal of Rochester's marriage proposal. Jane believes that "marrying" Rochester while he remains legally tied to Bertha would mean rendering herself a mistress and sacrificing her own integrity for the sake of emotional gratification. On the other hand, her life at Moor House tests her in the opposite manner. There, she enjoys economic independence and engages in worthwhile and useful work, teaching the poor; yet she lacks emotional sustenance. Although St. John proposes marriage, offering her a partnership built around a common purpose, Jane knows their marriage would remain loveless.

Nonetheless, the events of Jane's stay at Moor House are necessary tests of Jane's autonomy. Only after proving her self-sufficiency to herself can she marry Rochester and not be asymmetrically dependent upon him as her "master." The marriage can be one between equals. As Jane says: "I am my husband's life as fully as he is mine. . . . To be together is for us to be at once as free as in solitude, as gay as in company. . . . We are precisely suited in character—perfect concord is the result" (Chapter 38).

Religion

Throughout the novel, Jane struggles to find the right balance between moral duty and earthly pleasure, between obligation to her spirit and attention to her body. She encounters three main religious figures: Mr. Brocklehurst, Helen Burns, and St. John Rivers. Each represents a model of religion that Jane ultimately rejects as she forms her own ideas about faith and principle, and their practical consequences.

Mr. Brocklehurst illustrates the dangers and hypocrisies that Charlotte Brontë perceived in the nineteenth-century Evangelical movement. Mr. Brocklehurst adopts the rhetoric of Evangelicalism when he claims to be purging his students of pride, but his method of subjecting them to various privations and humiliations, like when he orders that the naturally curly hair of one of Jane's classmates be cut so as to lie straight, is entirely un-Christian. Of course, Brocklehurst's proscriptions are difficult to follow, and his hypocritical support of his own luxuriously wealthy family at the expense of the Lowood students shows Brontë's wariness of the Evangelical movement. Helen Burns's meek and forbearing mode of Christianity, on the other hand, is too passive for Jane to adopt as her own, although she loves and admires Helen for it.

Many chapters later, St. John Rivers provides another model of Christian behavior. His is a Christianity of ambition, glory, and extreme self-importance. St. John urges Jane to sacrifice her emotional deeds for the fulfillment of her moral duty, offering her a way of life that would require her to be disloyal to her own self.

Although Jane ends up rejecting all three models of religion, she does not abandon morality, spiritualism, or a belief in a Christian God. When her wedding is interrupted, she prays to God for solace (Chapter 26). As she wanders the heath, poor and starving, she puts her survival in the hands of God (Chapter 28). She strongly objects to Rochester's lustful immorality, and she refuses to consider living with him while church and state still deem him married to another woman. Even so, Jane can barely bring herself to leave the only love she has ever known. She credits God with helping her to escape what she knows would have been an immoral life (Chapter 27).

Jane ultimately finds a comfortable middle ground. Her spiritual understanding is not hateful and oppressive like Brocklehurst's, nor does it require retreat from the everyday world as Helen's and St. John's religions do. For Jane, religion helps curb immoderate passions, and it spurs one on to worldly efforts and achievements. These achievements include full self-knowledge and complete faith in God.

Social Class

Jane Eyre is critical of Victorian England's strict social hierarchy. Brontë's exploration of the complicated social position of governesses is perhaps the novel's most important treatment of this theme. Like Heathcliff in *Wuthering Heights,* Jane is a figure of ambiguous class standing and, consequently, a source of extreme tension for the characters around her. Jane's manners, sophistication, and education are those of an aristocrat, because Victorian governesses, who tutored children in etiquette as well as academics, were expected to possess the "culture" of the aristocracy. Yet, as paid employees, they were more or less treated as servants; thus, Jane remains penniless and powerless while at Thornfield. Jane's understanding of the double standard crystallizes when she becomes aware of her feelings for Rochester; she is his intellectual, but not his social, equal. Even before the crisis surrounding Bertha Mason, Jane is hesitant to marry Rochester because she senses that she would feel indebted to him for "condescending" to marry her. Jane's distress, which appears most strongly in Chapter 17, seems to be Brontë's critique of Victorian class attitudes.

Jane herself speaks out against class prejudice at certain moments in the book. For example, in Chapter 23 she chastises Rochester: "Do you think, because I am poor, obscure, plain, and little, I am soulless and heartless? You think wrong!—I have as much soul as you—and full as much heart! And if God had gifted me with some beauty and much wealth, I should have made it as hard for you to leave me, as it is now for me to leave you." However, it is also important to note that nowhere in *Jane Eyre* are society's boundaries bent. Ultimately, Jane is only able to marry Rochester as his equal because she has almost magically come into her own inheritance from her uncle.

Gender Relations

Jane struggles continually to achieve equality and to overcome oppression. In addition to class hierarchy, she must fight against patriarchal domination—against those who believe women to be inferior to men and try to treat them as such. Three central male figures threaten her desire for equality and dignity: Mr. Brocklehurst, Edward Rochester, and St. John Rivers. All three are misogynistic on some level. Each tries to keep Jane in a submissive position, where she is unable to express her own thoughts and feelings. In her quest for independence and self-knowledge, Jane must escape Brocklehurst, reject St. John, and come to Rochester only after ensuring that they may marry as equals. This last condition is met once Jane proves herself able to function, through the time she spends at Moor House, in a community and in a family. She will not depend solely on Rochester for love and she can be financially independent. Furthermore, Rochester is blind at the novel's end and thus dependent upon Jane to be his "prop and guide." In Chapter 12, Jane articulates what was for her time a radically feminist philosophy:

> Women are supposed to be very calm generally: but women feel just as men feel; they need exercise for their faculties, and a field for their efforts as much as their brothers do; they suffer from too rigid a restraint, too absolute a stagnation, precisely as men would suffer; and it is narrow-minded in their more privileged fellow-creatures to say that they ought to confine themselves to making puddings and knitting stockings, to playing on the piano and embroidering bags. It is thoughtless to condemn them, or laugh at them, if they seek to do more or learn more than custom has pronounced necessary for their sex.

MOTIFS

Motifs are recurring structures, contrasts, or literary devices that can help to develop and inform the text's major themes.

Fire and Ice

Fire and ice appear throughout *Jane Eyre*. The former represents Jane's passions, anger, and spirit, while the latter symbolizes the oppressive forces trying to extinguish Jane's vitality. Fire is also a metaphor for Jane, as the narrative repeatedly associates her with images of fire, brightness, and warmth. In Chapter 4, she likens her mind to "a ridge of lighted heath, alive, glancing, devouring." We can recognize Jane's kindred spirits by their similar links to fire; thus we read of Rochester's "flaming and flashing" eyes (Chapter 25). After he has been blinded, his face is compared to "a lamp quenched, waiting to be relit" (Chapter 37).

Images of ice and cold, often appearing in association with barren landscapes or seascapes, symbolize emotional desolation, loneliness, or even death. The "death-white realms" of the arctic that Bewick describes in his *History of British Birds* parallel Jane's physical and spiritual isolation at Gateshead (Chapter 1). Lowood's freezing temperatures—for example, the frozen pitchers of water that greet the girls each morning—mirror Jane's sense of psychological exile. After the interrupted wedding to Rochester, Jane describes her state of mind: "A Christmas frost had come at mid-summer: a white December storm had whirled over June; ice glazed the ripe apples, drifts crushed the blowing roses; on hay-field and corn-field lay a frozen shroud . . . and the woods, which twelve hours since waved leafy and fragrant as groves between the tropics, now spread, waste, wild, and white as pine-forests in wintry Norway. My hopes were all dead. . . ." (Chapter 26). Finally, at Moor House, St. John's frigidity and stiffness are established through comparisons with ice and cold rock. Jane writes: "By degrees, he acquired a certain influence over me that took away my liberty of mind. . . . I fell under a freezing spell"(Chapter 34). When St. John proposes marriage to Jane, she concludes that "[a]s his curate, his comrade, all would be right. . . . But as his wife—at his side always, and always restrained, and always checked—forced to keep the fire of my nature continually low, to compel it to burn inwardly and never utter a cry, though the imprisoned flame consumed vital after vital—*this* would be unendurable" (Chapter 34).

Substitute Mothers

Poet and critic Adrienne Rich has noted that Jane encounters a series of nurturing and strong women on whom she can model herself, or to whom she can look for comfort and guidance: these women serve as mother-figures to the orphaned Jane.

The first such figure that Jane encounters is the servant Bessie, who soothes Jane after her trauma in the red-room and teaches her to find comfort in stories and songs. At Lowood, Jane meets Miss Temple, who has no power in the world at large, but possesses great spiritual strength and charm. Not only does she shelter Jane from pain, she also encourages her intellectual development. Of Miss Temple, Jane writes: "she had stood by me in the stead of mother, governess, and latterly, companion" (Chapter 10). Jane also finds a comforting model in Helen Burns, whose lessons in stamina teach Jane about self-worth and the power of faith.

After Jane and Rochester's wedding is cancelled, Jane finds comfort in the moon, which appears to her in a dream as a symbol of the matriarchal spirit. Jane sees the moon as "a white human form" shining in the sky, "inclining a glorious brow earthward." She tells us: "It spoke to my spirit: immeasurably distant was the tone, yet so near, it whispered in my heart—"My daughter, flee temptation." Jane answers, "Mother, I will" (Chapter 27). Waking from the dream, Jane leaves Thornfield.

Jane finds two additional mother-figures in the characters of Diana and Mary Rivers. Rich points out that the sisters bear the names of the pagan and Christian versions of "the Great Goddess": Diana, the Virgin huntress, and Mary, the Virgin Mother. Unmarried and independent, the Rivers sisters love learning and reciting poetry and live as intellectual equals with their brother St. John.

SYMBOLS

Symbols are objects, characters, figures, or colors used to represent abstract ideas or concepts.

Bertha Mason

Bertha Mason is a complex presence in *Jane Eyre*. She impedes Jane's happiness, but she also catalyses the growth of Jane's self-understanding. The mystery surrounding Bertha establishes suspense and terror to the plot and the atmosphere. Further, Bertha serves as a remnant and reminder of Rochester's youthful libertinism.

Yet Bertha can also be interpreted as a symbol. Some critics have read her as a statement about the way Britain feared and psychologically "locked away" the other cultures it encountered at the height of its imperialism. Others have seen her as a symbolic representation of the "trapped" Victorian wife, who is expected never to travel or work outside the house and becomes ever more frenzied as she finds no outlet for her frustration and anxiety. Within the story, then, Bertha's insanity could serve as a warning to Jane of what complete surrender to Rochester could bring about.

One could also see Bertha as a manifestation of Jane's subconscious feelings—specifically, of her rage against oppressive social and gender norms. Jane declares her love for Rochester, but she also secretly fears marriage to him and feels the need to rage against the imprisonment it could become for her. Jane never manifests this fear or anger, but Bertha does. Thus Bertha tears up the bridal veil, and it is Bertha's existence that indeed stops the wedding from going forth. And, when Thornfield comes to represent a state of servitude and submission for Jane, Bertha burns it to the ground. Throughout the novel, Jane describes her inner spirit as fiery, her inner landscape as a "ridge of lighted heath" (Chapter 4). Bertha seems to be the outward manifestation of Jane's interior fire. Bertha expresses the feelings that Jane must keep in check.

The Red-Room

The red-room can be viewed as a symbol of what Jane must overcome in her struggles to find freedom, happiness, and a sense of belonging. In the red-room, Jane's position of exile and imprisonment first becomes clear. Although Jane is eventually freed from the room, she continues to be socially ostracized, financially trapped, and excluded from love; her sense of independence and her freedom of self-expression are constantly threatened.

The red-room's importance as a symbol continues throughout the novel. It reappears as a memory whenever Jane makes a connection between her current situation and that first feeling of being ridiculed. Thus she recalls the room when she is humiliated at Lowood. She also thinks of the room on the night that she decides to leave Thornfield after Rochester has tried to convince her to become an undignified mistress. Her destitute condition upon her departure from Thornfield also threatens emotional and intellectual imprisonment, as does St. John's marriage proposal. Only after Jane has asserted herself, gained financial independence, and found a spiritual family—which turns out to be her real family—can she wed Rochester and find freedom in and through marriage.

CHAPTERS 1–4

Summary

Chapter 1

The novel opens on a dreary November afternoon at Gateshead, the home of the wealthy Reed family. A young girl named Jane Eyre sits in the drawing room reading Bewick's *History of British Birds*. Jane's aunt, Mrs. Reed, has forbidden her niece to play with her cousins Eliza, Georgiana, and the bullying John. John chides Jane for being a lowly orphan who is only permitted to live with the Reeds because of his mother's charity. John then hurls a book at the young girl, pushing her to the end of her patience. Jane finally erupts, and the two cousins fight. Mrs. Reed holds Jane responsible for the scuffle and sends her to the "red-room"—the frightening chamber in which her Uncle Reed died—as punishment.

Chapter 2

Two servants, Miss Abbott and Bessie Lee, escort Jane to the red-room, and Jane resists them with all of her might. Once locked in the room, Jane catches a glimpse of her ghastly figure in the mirror, and, shocked by her meager presence, she begins to reflect on the events that have led her to such a state. She remembers her kind Uncle Reed bringing her to Gateshead after her parents' death, and she recalls his dying command that his wife promise to raise Jane as one of her own. Suddenly, Jane is struck with the impression that her Uncle Reed's ghost is in the room, and she imagines that he has come to take revenge on his wife for breaking her promise. Jane cries out in terror, but her aunt believes that she is just trying to escape her punishment, and she ignores her pleas. Jane faints in exhaustion and fear.

Chapter 3

When she wakes, Jane finds herself in her own bedroom, in the care of Mr. Lloyd, the family's kind apothecary. Bessie is also present, and she expresses disapproval of her mistress's treatment of Jane. Jane remains in bed the following day, and Bessie sings her a song. Mr. Lloyd speaks with Jane about her life at Gateshead, and he suggests to Jane's aunt that the girl be sent away to school, where she might find happiness. Jane is cautiously excited at the possibility of leaving Gateshead.

Soon after her own reflections on the past in the red-room, Jane learns more of her history when she overhears a conversation between Bessie and Miss Abbott. Jane's mother was a member of the wealthy Reed family, which strongly disapproved of Jane's father, an impoverished clergyman. When they married, Jane's wealthy maternal grandfather wrote his daughter out of his will. Not long after Jane was born, Jane's parents died from typhus, which Jane's father contracted while caring for the poor.

Chapter 4

"I am glad you are no relation of mine. I will never call you aunt again as long as I live. I will never come to visit you when I am grown up; and if any one asks me how I liked you, and how you treated me, I will say the very thought of you makes me sick. . . ."

About two months have passed, and Jane has been enduring even crueler treatment from her aunt and cousins while anxiously waiting for the arrangements to be made for her schooling. Now Jane is finally told she may attend the girls' school Lowood, and she is introduced to Mr. Brocklehurst, the stern-faced man who runs the school. Mr. Brocklehurst abrasively questions Jane about religion, and he reacts with indignation when she declares that she finds the psalms uninteresting. Jane's aunt warns Mr. Brocklehurst that the girl also has a propensity for lying, a piece of information that Mr. Brocklehurst says he intends to publicize to Jane's teachers upon her arrival. When Mr. Brocklehurst leaves, Jane is so hurt by her aunt's accusation that she cannot stop herself from defending herself to her aunt. Mrs. Reed, for once, seems to concede defeat. Shortly thereafter, Bessie tells Jane that she prefers her to the Reed children. Before Jane leaves for school, Bessie tells her stories and sings her lovely songs.

Analysis

In the early chapters, Brontë establishes the young Jane's character through her confrontations with John and Mrs. Reed, in which Jane's good-hearted but strong-willed determination and integrity become apparent. These chapters also establish the novel's mood. Beginning with Jane's experience in the red-room in Chapter 2, we sense a palpable atmosphere of mystery and the supernatural. Like Emily Brontë's *Wuthering Heights*, *Jane Eyre* draws a great deal of its stylistic inspiration from the Gothic novels that were in vogue during the late eighteenth and early nineteenth centuries. These books depicted remote, desolate landscapes, crumbling ruins, and supernatural events, all of which were designed to create a sense of psychological suspense and horror. While *Jane Eyre* is certainly not a horror novel, and its intellectually ambitious criticisms of society make it far more than a typical Gothic romance, it is Brontë's employment of Gothic conventions that gives her novel popular as well as intellectual appeal.

From its beginning, *Jane Eyre* explores and challenges the social preconceptions of nineteenth-century Victorian society. Themes of social class, gender relations, and injustice predominate throughout. Jane Eyre begins her story as an orphan raised by a wealthy and cultivated family, and this ambiguous social standing motivates much of the novel's internal tension and conflict. Jane's education and semi-aristocratic lifestyle are those of the upper class, but she has no money. As a penniless orphan forced to live on the charity of others, Jane is a kind of second-class citizen. In some ways she is below even the servants, who certainly have no obligation to treat her respectfully. The tensions of this contradiction emerge in the very first chapter of the novel, when Jane suffers teasing and punishment at the hands of John Reed and his hateful mother. Jane's banishment to the red-room exemplifies her inferior position with regard to the rest of the members of the Reed household.

The red-room is the first in a series of literal and metaphorical imprisonments in the novel. Although Jane's imprisonment in the red-room is real, she will encounter spiritual, intellectual, and emotional imprisonment throughout the book. The rigid Victorian hierarchies of social class and gender will pose challenges to her freedom of movement and personal growth, and corrupt morals and religion will also constitute menaces to her ability to realize her dreams for herself. Jane will even come to fear "enslavement" to her own passions. At the same time, the red-room is also symbolic of Jane's feeling of isolation with respect to every community: she is "locked in," but she is also, in a sense, "locked out." Again, class and gender hierarchies will contribute to Jane's sense of exile. For example, her position as a governess at Thornfield once again situates her in a strange borderland between the upper class and the servant class, so that she feels part of neither group.

CHAPTERS 5–10

Summary

Chapter 5

Four days after meeting Mr. Brocklehurst, Jane boards the 6 A.M. coach and travels alone to Lowood. When she arrives at the school, the day is dark and rainy, and she is led through a grim building that will be her new home. The following day, Jane is introduced to her classmates and learns the daily routine, which keeps the girls occupied from before dawn until dinner. Miss Temple, the superintendent of the school, is very kind, while one of Jane's teachers, Miss Scatcherd, is unpleasant, particularly in her harsh treatment of a young student named Helen Burns. Jane and Helen befriend one another, and Jane learns from Helen that Lowood is a charity school maintained for female orphans, which means that the Reeds have paid nothing to put her there. She also learns that Mr. Brocklehurst oversees every aspect of its operation: even Miss Temple must answer to him.

Chapter 6

On Jane's second morning at Lowood, the girls are unable to wash, as the water in their pitchers is frozen. Jane quickly learns that life at the school is harsh. The girls are underfed, overworked, and forced to sit still during seemingly endless sermons. Still, she takes comfort in her new friendship with Helen, who impresses Jane with her expansive knowledge and her ability to patiently endure even the cruelest treatment from

Miss Scatcherd. Helen tells Jane that she practices a doctrine of Christian endurance, which means loving her enemies and accepting her privation. Jane disagrees strongly with such meek tolerance of injustice, but Helen takes no heed of Jane's arguments. Helen is self-critical only because she sometimes fails to live up to her ascetic standards: she believes that she is a poor student and chastises herself for daydreaming about her home and family when she should be concentrating on her studies.

Chapter 7

For most of Jane's first month at Lowood, Mr. Brocklehurst spends his time away from the school. When he returns, Jane becomes quite nervous because she remembers his promise to her aunt, Mrs. Reed, to warn the school about Jane's supposed habit of lying. When Jane inadvertently drops her slate in Mr. Brocklehurst's presence, he is furious and tells her she is careless. He orders Jane to stand on a stool while he tells the school that she is a liar, and he forbids the other students to speak to her for the rest of the day. Helen makes Jane's day of humiliation endurable by providing her friend with silent consolation—she covertly smiles at Jane every time she passes by.

Chapter 8

Finally, at five o'clock, the students disperse, and Jane collapses to the floor. Deeply ashamed, she is certain that her reputation at Lowood has been ruined, but Helen assures her that most of the girls felt more pity for Jane than revulsion at her alleged deceitfulness. Jane tells Miss Temple that she is not a liar, and relates the story of her tormented childhood at Gateshead. Miss Temple seems to believe Jane and writes to Mr. Lloyd requesting confirmation of Jane's account of events. Miss Temple offers Jane and Helen tea and seed cake, endearing herself even further to Jane. When Mr. Lloyd's letter arrives and corroborates Jane's story, Miss Temple publicly declares Jane to be innocent. Relieved and contented, Jane devotes herself to her studies. She excels at drawing and makes progress in French.

Chapter 9

In the spring, life at Lowood briefly seems happier, but the damp forest dell in which the school resides is a breeding-ground for typhus, and in the warm temperatures more than half the girls fall ill with the disease. Jane remains healthy and spends her time playing outdoors with a new friend, Mary Ann Wilson. Helen is sick, but not with typhus—Jane learns the horrific news that her friend is dying of consumption. One evening, Jane sneaks into Miss Temple's room to see Helen one last time. Helen promises Jane that she feels little pain and is happy to be leaving the world's suffering behind. Jane takes Helen into her arms, and the girls fall asleep. During the night, Helen dies. Her grave is originally unmarked, but fifteen years after her death, a gray marble tablet is placed over the spot (presumably by Jane), bearing the single word *Resurgam*, Latin for "I shall rise again."

Chapter 10

After Mr. Brocklehurst's negligent treatment of the girls at Lowood is found to be one of the causes of the typhus epidemic, a new group of overseers is brought in to run the school. Conditions improve dramatically for the young girls, and Jane excels in her studies for the next six years. After spending two more years at Lowood as a teacher, Jane decides she is ready for a change, partly because Miss Temple gets married and leaves the school. She advertises in search of a post as a governess and accepts a position at a manor called Thornfield.

Before leaving, Jane receives a visit from Bessie, who tells her what has happened at Gateshead since Jane departed for Lowood. Georgiana attempted to run away in secret with a man named Lord Edwin Vere, but Eliza foiled the plan by revealing it to Mrs. Reed. John has fallen into a life of debauchery and dissolution. Bessie also tells Jane that her father's brother, John Eyre, appeared at Gateshead seven years ago, looking for Jane. He did not have the time to travel to Lowood and went away to Madeira (a Portuguese island west of Morocco) in search of wealth. Jane and Bessie part ways, Bessie returning to Gateshead, and Jane leaving for her new life at Thornfield.

Analysis

This section details Jane's experiences at Lowood, from her first day at the school to her final one some nine years later. Jane's early years at Lowood prove to be a period of considerable tribulation, as she endures harsh conditions, cruel teachers, and the tyranny of Mr. Brocklehurst.

Moreover, the harsh conditions she experiences as a student at Lowood show us that, despite Jane's intelligence, talent, and self-assurance, she is merely a burden in the eyes of society, because she is poor.

The most important thematic elements in this section are the contrasting modes of religious thought represented by Mr. Brocklehurst and Helen Burns. Mr. Brocklehurst is a religious hypocrite, supporting his own luxuriously wealthy family at the expense of the Lowood students and using his "piety" as an instrument of power over the lower-class girls at Lowood. He claims that he is purging his students of pride by subjecting them to various privations and humiliations: for example, he orders that the naturally curly hair of one of Jane's classmates be cut so as to lie straight.

The angelic Helen Burns and her doctrine of endurance represent a religious position that contrasts with Mr. Brocklehurst's. Utterly passive and accepting of any abjection, Helen embodies rather than preaches the Christian ideas of love and forgiveness. But neither form of religion satisfies Jane, who, because of her strong sensitivity to indignities and injustices, reviles Brocklehurst's shallow devotional displays and fails to understand Helen Burns's passivity. As Jane herself declares: "when we are struck at without a reason, we should strike back again very hard . . . so as to teach the person who struck us never to do it again" (Chapter 6). Helen's doctrine of endurance and love is incompatible with Jane's belief in fairness and self-respect.

CHAPTERS 11–16

Summary

Chapter 11

Jane's driver is late picking her up from the station at Millcote. When she finally arrives at Thornfield it is nighttime. Although she cannot distinguish much of the house's facade from among the shadows, she finds the interior "cosy and agreeable." Mrs. Fairfax, a prim, elderly woman, is waiting for Jane. It turns out that Mrs. Fairfax is not, as Jane had assumed from their correspondence, the owner of Thornfield, but rather the housekeeper. Thornfield's owner, Mr. Rochester, travels regularly and leaves much of the manor's management to Mrs. Fairfax. Jane learns that she will be tutoring Adèle, an eight-year-old French girl whose mother was a singer and dancer. Mrs. Fairfax also tells Jane about Rochester, saying that he is an eccentric man whose family has a history of extreme and violent behavior. Suddenly, Jane hears a peal of strange, eerie laughter echoing through the house, and Mrs. Fairfax summons someone named Grace, whom she orders to make less noise and to "remember directions." When Grace leaves, Mrs. Fairfax explains that she is a rather unbalanced and unpredictable seamstress who works in the house.

Chapter 12

It is in vain to say human beings ought to be satisfied with tranquility: they must have action; and they will make it if they cannot find it. Millions are condemned to a stiller doom than mine, and millions are in silent revolt against their lot.

Jane finds life at Thornfield pleasant and comfortable. Adèle proves to be exuberant and intelligent, though spoiled and at times a bit petulant. Nonetheless, Jane is frequently restless and collects her thoughts while pacing Thornfield's top-story passageway. One evening a few months after her arrival at Thornfield, Jane is alone watching the moon rise when she perceives a horse approaching. It calls to her mind the story Bessie once told her of a spirit called a Gytrash, which disguises itself as a mule, dog, or horse to frighten "belated travellers." Oddly enough, a dog then appears as well. Once she realizes that the horse has a rider, the uncanny moment ceases. Just after the horse passes her, it slips on a patch of ice, and its rider tumbles to the ground. Jane helps the man rise to his feet and introduces herself to him. She observes that he has a dark face, stern features, and a heavy brow. He is not quite middle-aged. Upon reentering Thornfield, Jane goes to Mrs. Fairfax's room and sees the same dog—Pilot—resting on the rug. A servant answers Jane's queries, explaining that the dog belongs to Mr. Rochester, who has just returned home with a sprained ankle, having fallen from his horse.

Chapter 13

The day following his arrival, Mr. Rochester invites Jane and Adèle to have tea with him. He is abrupt and rather cold toward both of them, although he seems charmed by Jane's drawings, which he asks to see. When Jane mentions to Mrs. Fairfax that she finds Rochester "changeful and abrupt," Mrs. Fairfax suggests that his mannerisms are the result of a difficult personal history. Rochester was something of a family outcast, and when his father died, his older brother inherited Thornfield. Rochester has been Thornfield's proprietor for nine years, since the death of his brother.

Chapter 14

Jane sees little of Rochester during his first days at Thornfield. One night, however, in his "after-dinner mood," Rochester sends for Jane and Adèle. He gives Adèle the present she has been anxiously awaiting, and while Adèle plays, Rochester is uncharacteristically chatty with Jane. When Rochester asks Jane whether she thinks him handsome, she answers "no" without thinking, and from Rochester's voluble reaction Jane concludes that he is slightly drunk. Rochester's command that she converse with him makes Jane feel awkward, especially because he goes on to argue that her relationship to him is not one of servitude. Their conversation turns to the concepts of sin, forgiveness, and redemption. When Adèle mentions her mother, Jane is intrigued, and Rochester promises to explain more about the situation on a future occasion.

Chapter 15

A while later, Rochester fulfills his promise to Jane to tell her about his and Adèle's pasts. He had a long affair with Adèle's mother, the French singer and dancer named Celine Varens. When he discovered that Celine was engaged in relations with another man, Rochester ended the relationship. Rochester has always denied Celine's claim that Adèle is his daughter, noting that the child looks utterly unlike him. Even so, when Celine abandoned her daughter, Rochester brought Adèle to England so that she would be properly cared for.

Jane lies awake brooding about the strange insights she has gained into her employer's past. She hears what sound like fingers brushing against the walls, and an eerie laugh soon emanates from the hallway. She hears a door opening and hurries out of her room to see smoke coming from Rochester's door. Jane dashes into his room and finds his bed curtains ablaze. She douses the bed with water, saving Rochester's life. Strangely, Rochester's reaction is to visit the third floor of the house. When he returns, he says mysteriously, "I have found it all out, it is just as I thought." He inquires whether Jane has ever heard the eerie laughter before, and she answers that she has heard Grace Poole laugh in the same way. "Just so. Grace Poole—you have guessed it," Rochester confirms. He thanks Jane for saving his life and cautions her to tell no one about the details of the night's events. He sleeps on the library sofa for the remainder of the night.

Chapter 16

The next morning, Jane is shocked to learn that the near tragedy of the night before has caused no scandal. The servants believe Rochester to have fallen asleep with a lit candle by his bed, and even Grace Poole shows no sign of guilt or remorse. Jane cannot imagine why an attempted murderer is allowed to continue working at Thornfield. She realizes that she is beginning to have feelings for Rochester and is disappointed that he will be away from Thornfield for several days. He has left to attend a party where he will be in the company of Blanche Ingram, a beautiful lady whom Jane has met before. Jane scolds herself for being disappointed by the news, and she resolves to restrain her flights of imaginative fancy by comparing her own portrait to one she has drawn of Blanche Ingram, noting how much plainer she is than the beautiful Blanche.

Analysis

This section marks the third phase of Jane's life, in which she begins her career as a governess and travels to Thornfield, where the principal incidents of her story take place. By linking Jane's stages of development to the various institutions or geographic locations with which she is involved (Gateshead, Lowood, Thornfield, Moor House, and Ferndean, in order), the book positions itself among a literary genre known as the *Bildungsroman.*

The *Bildungsroman,* a novel that details the growth and development of a main character through several periods of life, began as a German genre in the seventeenth century, but by the mid-1800s had become firmly established in England as well. Such important Victorian novels as *David Copperfield* base themselves on this form, which continues as an important literary sub-genre even today. The *Bildungsroman* typically told the story of a man growing from boyhood to adulthood; Charlotte Brontë's appropriation of the form for her heroine represents one of the many ways in which her novel challenges the accepted Victorian conceptions of gender hierarchy, making the statement that a woman's inner development merits as much attention and analysis as that of a man. Still, although Jane herself and *Jane Eyre* as a novel are often identified as important early figures in the feminist movement, Jane experiences much inner questioning regarding her gender role; she is not a staunch and confident feminist at all times. That is, while Jane is possessed of an immense integrity and a determination to succeed on her own terms, her failure to conform to ideals of female beauty nonetheless troubles her and makes her question herself.

Just as Jane's time at Lowood involved a number of elements taken from Charlotte Brontë's own life, so too is Jane's career as a governess based in part on Brontë's short-lived position as a governess in the late 1830s. In many ways, Brontë's exploration of the role of the governess represents the novel's most important and challenging treatment of the theme of social class. Just as Emily Brontë does with Heathcliff in *Wuthering Heights*, Charlotte Brontë makes Jane a figure of ambiguous class standing. Consequently, she is a source of extreme tension for the characters around her. But while Heathcliff (an orphan like Jane) achieves wealth and power without achieving education or social grace, Jane acquires the manners, sophistication, and education of an aristocrat while remaining penniless and powerless. Such was the role of the governess: brought into wealthy Victorian households as the children's private tutors in both academics and etiquette, governesses were expected to possess the demeanor of the aristocracy; but as paid employees, they were in many ways treated merely as servants. Jane begins to experience this tension as soon as she notices her emerging feelings for Rochester. Though she is in some ways his social equal, she is also his servant, and thus she cannot believe that he could ever fall in love with her.

CHAPTERS 17–21

Summary

Chapter 17

Rochester has been gone for a week, and Jane is dismayed to learn that he may choose to depart for continental Europe without returning to Thornfield—according to Mrs. Fairfax, he could be gone for more than a year. A week later, however, Mrs. Fairfax receives word that Rochester will arrive in three days with a large group of guests. While she waits, Jane continues to be amazed by the apparently normal relations the strange, self–isolated Grace Poole enjoys with the rest of the staff. Jane also overhears a conversation in which a few of the servants discuss Grace's high pay, and Jane is certain that she doesn't know the entire truth about Grace Poole's role at Thornfield.

Rochester arrives at last, accompanied by a party of elegant and aristocratic guests. Jane is forced to join the group but spends the evening watching them from a window seat. Blanche Ingram and her mother are among the party's members, and they treat Jane with disdain and cruelty. Jane tries to leave the party, but Rochester stops her. He grudgingly allows her to go when he sees the tears brimming in her eyes. He informs her that she must come into the drawing room every evening during his guests' stay at Thornfield. As they part, Rochester nearly lets slip more than he intends. "Good-night, my—" he says, before biting his lip.

Chapter 18

The guests stay at Thornfield for several days. Rochester and Blanche compete as a team at charades. From watching their interaction, Jane believes that they will be married soon though they do not seem to love one another. Blanche would be marrying Rochester for his wealth, and he for her beauty and her social position. One day, a strange man named Mr. Mason arrives at Thornfield. Jane dislikes him at once because of his vacant eyes and his slowness, but she learns from him that Rochester once lived in the West Indies, as he himself has done. One evening, a gypsy woman comes to Thornfield to tell the guests' fortunes. Blanche

Ingram goes first, and when she returns from her talk with the gypsy woman she looks keenly disappointed.

Chapter 19

Jane goes in to the library to have her fortune read, and after overcoming her skepticism, she finds herself entranced by the old woman's speech. The gypsy woman seems to know a great deal about Jane and tells her that she is very close to happiness. She also says that she told Blanche Ingram that Rochester was not as wealthy as he seemed, thereby accounting for Blanche's sullen mood. As the woman reads Jane's fortune, her voice slowly deepens, and Jane realizes that the gypsy is Rochester in disguise. Jane reproaches Rochester for tricking her and remembers thinking that Grace Poole might have been the gypsy. When Rochester learns that Mr. Mason has arrived, he looks troubled.

Chapter 20

The same night, Jane is startled by a sudden cry for help. She hurries into the hallway, where Rochester assures everyone that a servant has merely had a nightmare. After everyone returns to bed, Rochester knocks on Jane's door. He tells her that he can use her help and asks whether she is afraid of blood. He leads her to the third story of the house and shows her Mr. Mason, who has been stabbed in the arm. Rochester asks Jane to stanch the wound and then leaves, ordering Mason and Jane not to speak to one another. In the silence, Jane gazes at the image of the apostles and Christ's crucifixion that is painted on the cabinet across from her. Rochester returns with a surgeon, and as the men tend to Mason's wounds, Rochester sends Jane to find a potion downstairs. He gives some of it to Mason, saying that it will give him heart for an hour. Once Mason is gone, Jane and Rochester stroll in the orchard, and Rochester tells Jane a hypothetical story about a young man who commits a "capital error" in a foreign country and proceeds to lead a life of dissipation in an effort to "obtain relief." The young man then hopes to redeem himself and live morally with a wife, but convention prevents him from doing so. He asks whether the young man would be justified in "overleaping an obstacle of custom." Jane's reply is that such a man should look to God for his redemption, not to another person. Rochester—who obviously has been describing his own situation—asks Jane to reassure him that marrying Blanche would bring him salvation. He then hurries away before she has a chance to answer.

Chapter 21

Jane has heard that it is a bad omen to dream of children, and now she has dreams on seven consecutive nights involving babies. She learns that her cousin John Reed has committed suicide, and that her aunt, Mrs. Reed, has suffered a stroke and is nearing death. Jane goes to Gateshead, where she is reunited with Bessie. She also sees her cousins Eliza and Georgiana. Eliza is plain and plans to enter a convent, while Georgiana is as beautiful as ever. Ever since Eliza ruined Georgiana's hopes of eloping with a young man, the two sisters have not gotten along. Jane tries to patch things up with Mrs. Reed, but the old woman is still full of hostility toward her late husband's favorite. One day, Mrs. Reed gives Jane a letter from her father's brother, John Eyre. He declares that he wishes to adopt Jane and bequeath her his fortune. The letter is three years old; out of malice, Mrs. Reed did not forward it to Jane when she received it. In spite of her aunt's behavior, Jane tries once more to smooth relations with the dying woman. But Mrs. Reed refuses, and, at midnight, she dies.

Analysis

Jane's situation in Chapter 17 manifests the uncomfortable position of governesses. Jane, forced to sit in the drawing room during Rochester's party, must endure Blanche Ingram's comments to her mother about the nature of governesses—"half of them detestable and the rest ridiculous, and all incubi." ("Incubi" is the plural of "incubus," an oppressive or nightmarish burden.)

By this stage of the story, the narrative has begun to focus increasingly on the potential relationship between Jane and Rochester. Blanche's presence, which threatens the possibility of a union between the two, adds tension to the plot. Blanche is not only a competitor for Jane, she is also a foil to her, as the two women differ in every respect. *Jane Eyre* never seems to possess the degree of romantic tension that runs throughout Emily Brontë's *Wuthering Heights* because the signs of Rochester's affection for Jane are recognizable early on. The most telling tip-off occurs at the end of Chapter 17, when Rochester nearly calls Jane "my love" before biting his tongue. The tension surrounding Jane's and

Rochester's relationship derives not from the question of whether Rochester loves Jane, but from whether he will be able to act upon his feelings. So far, two obstacles—Blanche and the dark secrets of Thornfield Hall—stand in Rochester's way.

These obstacles, and the potential marriage that they impede, constitute the romantic plot of *Jane Eyre*. As in many romances, the norms of society and the protagonists' conflicting personalities must either be changed or ignored in order for marriage to be possible. But Rochester's dark past, most importantly his secret marriage to Bertha, adds a Gothic element to the story. Unlike the marriage plot, which leads toward the public, communal event of a wedding, the "Gothic plot" of Rochester's struggle with his own past focuses on Rochester's private consciousness. The physical world of Thornfield Hall reflects his interior state—the house, the landscape, and Bertha can all be seen as external manifestations of his dangerous secrets. These Gothic elements suggest that the story will lead to death or madness rather than the happy occasion of a wedding.

Disguised as a gypsy woman, Rochester wields an almost magical power over Jane, and the scene reveals how much he controls her emotions at this stage of the novel. He also controls the plot, and his masquerading as a gypsy woman allows him to overcome the obstacle Blanche poses. Like the game of charades the group plays earlier, Rochester's disguised appearance suggests his disguised character. Mr. Mason's unexplained wounds, like the earlier mysterious fire in Rochester's bedroom, further the larger Gothic plot that will soon unfold. By allowing Jane upstairs to see Mason, Rochester seems to be inviting her to help cure the ills inflicted by Bertha, and he attempts for the first time to talk with Jane about his past as they take a walk together following Mason's stabbing. Although he speaks to Jane about his determination to redeem himself, his references to a grave error and a dissipated youth suggest that Jane risks great danger not only by continuing to live at Thornfield but by falling in love with him. Her emotional welfare as well as her physical welfare may soon be in jeopardy. Adèle and Bertha already serve as living legacies of Rochester's past licentiousness, and Jane could be next in line, as her prophetic dream seems to suggest.

CHAPTERS 22–25

Summary

Chapter 22

Jane remains at Gateshead for a month because Georgiana dreads being left alone with Eliza, with whom she does not get along. Eventually, Georgiana goes to London to live with her uncle, and Eliza joins a convent in France. Jane tells us that Eliza eventually becomes the Mother Superior of her convent, while Georgiana marries a wealthy man. At Gateshead, Jane receives a letter from Mrs. Fairfax, which says that Rochester's guests have departed and that Rochester has gone to London to buy a new carriage—a sure sign of his intention to marry Blanche. As Jane travels toward Thornfield, she anxiously anticipates seeing Rochester again, and yet she worries about what will become of her after his marriage. To her surprise, as she walks from the station at Millcote, Jane encounters Rochester. When he asks her why she has stayed away from Thornfield so long, she replies, still a bit bewildered, "I have been with my aunt, sir, who is dead." Rochester asks Jane whether she has heard about his new carriage, and he tells her: "You must see the carriage, Jane, and tell me if you don't think it will suit Mrs. Rochester exactly." After a few more words together, Jane surprises herself by expressing the happiness she feels in Rochester's presence: "I am strangely glad to get back again to you; and wherever you are is my home—my only home." Back at the manor, Mrs. Fairfax, Adèle, and the servants greet Jane warmly.

Chapter 23

After a blissful two weeks, Jane encounters Rochester in the gardens. He invites her to walk with him, and Jane, caught off guard, accepts. Rochester confides that he has finally decided to marry Blanche Ingram and tells Jane that he knows of an available governess position in Ireland that she could take. Jane expresses her distress at the great distance that separates Ireland from Thornfield. The two seat themselves on a bench at the foot of the chestnut tree, and Rochester says: "we will sit there in peace to-night, though we should never more be destined to sit there together." He tells Jane that he feels as though they are connected by a "cord of communion." Jane sobs—"for I could repress what I endured no longer," she tells us, "I was obliged to yield." Jane confesses her love for Rochester, and to her surprise, he asks her to be his wife. She suspects that he is teasing her, but he convinces her otherwise by admitting that he only brought up marrying Blanche in order to arouse Jane's jealousy. Convinced and elated, Jane accepts his proposal. A storm breaks, and the newly engaged couple hurries indoors through the rain. Rochester helps Jane out of her wet coat, and he seizes the opportunity to kiss her. Jane looks up to see Mrs. Fairfax watching, astonished. That night, a bolt of lightning splits the same chestnut tree under which Rochester and Jane had been sitting that evening.

Chapter 24

Preparations for Jane and Rochester's wedding do not run smoothly. Mrs. Fairfax treats Jane coldly because she doesn't realize that Jane was already engaged to Rochester when she allowed him to kiss her. But even after she learns the truth, Mrs. Fairfax maintains her disapproval of the marriage. Jane feels unsettled, almost fearful, when Rochester calls her by what will soon be her name, Jane Rochester. Jane explains that everything feels impossibly ideal, like a fairy-tale or a daydream. Rochester certainly tries to turn Jane into a Cinderella-like figure: he tells her he will dress her in jewels and in finery befitting her new social station, at which point Jane becomes terrified and self-protective. She has a premonitory feeling that the wedding will not happen, and she decides to write her uncle, John Eyre, who is in Madeira. Jane reasons that if John Eyre were to make her his heir, her inheritance might put her on more equal footing with Rochester, which would make her feel less uncomfortable about the marriage.

Chapter 25

The night before her wedding, Jane waits for Rochester, who has left Thornfield for the evening. She grows restless and takes a walk in the orchard, where she sees the now-split chestnut tree. When Rochester arrives, Jane tells him about strange events that have occurred in his absence. The preceding evening, Jane's wedding dress arrived, and underneath it was an expensive veil—Rochester's wedding gift to Jane. In the night, Jane had a strange dream, in which a little child cried in her arms as Jane tried to make her way toward Rochester on a long, winding road. Rochester dismisses the dream as insignificant, but then she tells him about a second dream. This time, Jane loses her balance and the child falls from her knee. The dream was so disturbing that it roused Jane from her sleep, and she perceived "a form" rustling in her closet. It turned out to be a strange, savage-looking woman, who took Jane's veil and tore it in two. Rochester tells her that the woman must have been Grace Poole and that what she experienced was really "half-dream, half-reality." He tells her that he will give her a full explanation of events after they have been married for one year and one day. Jane sleeps with Adèle for the evening and cries because she will soon have to leave the sleeping girl.

Analysis

After her stay at Gateshead, Jane comes to understand fully what Rochester and Thornfield mean to her. Having been acutely reminded of the abjection and cruelty she suffered during her childhood, Jane now realizes how different her life has become, how much she has gained and how much she has grown. In Rochester she has found someone she truly cares for—someone who, despite periodic shows of brusqueness, nevertheless continues to admire Jane and care for her tenderly. Moreover, Rochester gives her a true sense of belonging, something she has always lacked. As she tells him, "wherever you are is my home—my only home."

Although Rochester's declaration of love and marriage proposal make Jane exceedingly happy, she is also very apprehensive about the marriage. Her feelings of dread may stem in part from a subconscious intimation of Rochester's dark and horrible secret, which will be divulged in the next few chapters: the eerie laughter she has heard, the mysterious fire from which she rescued Rochester, the strange figure who tears Jane's wedding veil, and other smaller clues may have led Jane to make some subconscious conclusions about what she will consciously find out only later.

Another possibility is that Jane's misgivings stem from other concerns. She has always longed for freedom and escape, and marrying Rochester would be a form of tying herself down. Jane may worry that the marriage will encroach upon her autonomy, and even enforce her submission to Rochester. Not only would the marriage bring her into a relationship of responsibility and commitment to another person, it could cement her into a position of inferiority.

Jane's anxiety surfaces when Rochester tries to dress her in feminine finery. She reacts with revulsion, noting that she feels like a toy doll. Jane fears that Rochester may be trying to objectify her, that he sees her not as a human being with her own thoughts and feelings but as a plaything designed to cater to his fantasies and whims. Jane also worries about her financial inferiority: she hates the thought of marrying "above her station," as she does not want to feel that she somehow "owes" Rochester something for the fact that he has "deigned" to love her, as it were. She hates the thought that his love might be a "favor" to her.

Thus, Jane's feelings and desires for Rochester are tightly bound up with her feelings about her social position (her status as an employee and her experiences of economic dependence) and her position as a woman. She is very sensitive to the hierarchy and power dynamic implicit in marriage, and despite her statement that she is forced to "yield" to her feelings for Rochester, she does not desire the complete surrender that heroines in romance novels experience. The storybook wedding toward which these chapters appear to lead cannot succeed, because Jane will only be able to occupy the role of wife on her own, quite different, terms.

CHAPTER 26

Summary

Sophie helps Jane dress for the wedding, and Rochester and Jane walk to the church. Jane notes a pair of strangers reading the headstones in the churchyard cemetery. When Jane and Rochester enter the church, the two strangers are also present. When the priest asks if anyone objects to the ceremony, one of the strangers answers: "The marriage cannot go on: I declare the existence of an impediment." Rochester attempts to proceed with the ceremony, but the stranger explains that Rochester is already married—his wife is a Creole woman whom Rochester wed fifteen years earlier in Jamaica. The speaker explains that he is a solicitor from London, and he introduces himself as Mr. Briggs. He produces a signed letter from Richard Mason affirming that Rochester is married to

Mason's sister, Bertha. Mr. Mason himself then steps forward to corroborate the story. After a moment of inarticulate fury, Rochester admits that his wife is alive and that in marrying Jane he would have been knowingly taking a second wife. No one in the community knows of his wife because she is mad, and Rochester keeps her locked away under the care of Grace Poole. But, he promises them all, Jane is completely ignorant of Bertha's existence. He orders the crowd to come to Thornfield to see her, so that they may understand what impelled him to his present course of action.

At Thornfield, the group climbs to the third story. Rochester points out the room where Bertha bit and stabbed her brother, and then he lifts a tapestry to uncover a second door. Inside the hidden room is Bertha Mason, under the care of Grace Poole. Jane writes:

> In the deep shade, at the farther end of the room, a figure ran backwards and forwards. What it was, whether beast or human being, one could not, at first sight tell: it grovelled, seemingly, on all fours; it snatched and growled like some strange wild animal: but it was covered with clothing, and a quantity of dark, grizzled hair, wild as a mane, hid its head and face.

Bertha attempts to strangle Rochester, who reminds his audience, "this is the sole conjugal embrace I am ever to know." Jane leaves the room with Mason and Briggs, who tells her that he learned of her intent to marry Jane via a letter from Jane's uncle, John Eyre, to Mason. It turns out that the two men are acquaintances, and Mason had stopped in Madeira on his way back to Jamaica when John received Jane's letter. Approaching death, John asked Mason to hurry to England to save his niece. After the wedding crowd disperses, Jane locks herself in her room and plunges into an inexpressible grief. She thinks about the almost calm manner in which the morning's events unfolded and how it seems disproportionate to the immense effect those events will have on her life. She prays to God to be with her.

Analysis

The incident of the "madwoman in the attic" is probably the most famous in *Jane Eyre*, and it has given rise to innumerable interpretations and symbolic readings. For example, Bertha Mason could represent the horror of Victorian marriage. Rochester claims to have imprisoned her because she is mad, but it is easy to imagine an opposite relation of cause and effect, in which years of enforced imprisonment and isolation have made her violently insane or, at least, increased her insanity. Thus, the madwoman in the attic could represent the confining and repressive aspects of Victorian wifehood, suggesting that the lack of autonomy and freedom in marriage suffocates women, threatening their mental and emotional health. Bertha's tearing of Jane's wedding veil could be seen as symbolizing her revolt against the institution of marriage.

Another interpretation is that Rochester's marriage to Bertha represents the British Empire's cultural and economic exploitation of its colonial subjects. Briggs's letter states that Bertha's mother is a "creole," which could mean either that she is a person of European descent born in the colonies or that she is of black or mixed descent. In either case, Bertha might have evoked British anxieties about having to deal with the other cultures under Britain's dominion, and Bertha's imprisonment might signify Britain's attempt to control and contain the influence of these subject cultures by metaphorically "locking them in the attic."

Still another interpretation of Bertha is that she is a double for Jane herself, the embodiment of Jane's repressed fear and anger, both in regard to her specific situation and in regard to oppression. For although Jane declares her love for Rochester, her dreams and apprehensions suggest that she also secretly fears being married to him, perhaps even that she secretly wants to rage against the imprisonment that marriage could become for her. Although Jane does not manifest this fear or rage, Bertha does. Thus, Bertha tears the bridal veil, and it is Bertha's existence that stops the wedding from going forth.

Each of these arguments provides an interesting way of thinking about the text, but it is also important to recognize that Bertha does not function merely as a symbol. Her presence is also a gripping story element and a source of external psychological distress for Jane, from which Jane develops and grows. Similarly, Thornfield could be seen as "British Society at Large," but Thornfield is more than just an allegory. The relationships between Thornfield's inhabitants as well as its architecture and grounds are all important to Jane's story. Lastly, Jane herself, while possessing many proto-feminist viewpoints, is not simply a symbol for the "Victorian Woman." Her individual psychology cannot be read as representing the mindset of all Victorian women.

CHAPTERS 27–28

Summary

Chapter 27

After falling asleep for a short while, Jane awakes to the realization that she must leave Thornfield. When she steps out of her room, she finds Rochester waiting in a chair on the threshold. To Rochester's assurances that he never meant to wound her, and to his pleas of forgiveness, Jane is silent, although she confides to the reader that she forgave him on the spot. Jane suddenly feels faint, and Rochester carries her to the library to revive her. He then offers her a new proposal—to leave England with him for the South of France, where they will live together as husband and wife. Jane refuses, explaining that no matter how Rochester chooses to view the situation, she will never be more than a mistress to him while Bertha is alive. Rochester realizes that he must explain why he does not consider himself married, and he launches into the story of his past.

Unwilling to divide his property, Rochester's father left his entire estate to his other son, Rowland, and sent Rochester to Jamaica to marry Bertha, who was to inherit a massive fortune—30,000 pounds. Bertha was beautiful, and although she and Rochester spent hardly any time alone, the stimulated, dazzled, and ignorant youth believed himself to be in love and agreed to the marriage. Shortly after the wedding, Rochester learned that Bertha's mother was not, as he had been led to believe, dead, but mad and living in an insane asylum. Bertha's younger brother was a mute idiot. Rochester's father and brother had known about the family's unpromising genetic legacy, but they had promoted the marriage for the sake of the money. Bertha soon revealed herself to be coarse, perverse, and prone to violent outbreaks of temper and unhealthy indulgences. These excesses only hastened the approach of what had been lurking on her horizon already: absolute madness. By this time, Rochester's father and brother had died, so Rochester found himself all alone with a maniacal wife and a huge fortune. He considered killing himself but returned to England instead. He resolved to place Bertha at Thornfield

Hall "in safety and comfort: [to] shelter her degradation with secrecy, and leave her." Rochester then drifted around the continent from one city to the next, always in search of a woman to love. When he was met with disappointment, he sank into debauchery. He was always disappointed with his mistresses, because they were, as he puts it, "the next worse thing to buying a slave." Then he met Jane. Rochester retells the story of their introduction from his point of view, telling her that she enchanted him from the start.

Jane feels torn. She doesn't want to condemn Rochester to further misery, and a voice within her asks, "Who in the world cares for *you*?" Jane wonders how she could ever find another man who values her the way Rochester does, and whether, after a life of loneliness and neglect, she should leave the first man who has ever loved her. Yet her conscience tells her that she will respect herself all the more if she bears her suffering alone and does what she believes to be right. She tells Rochester that she must go, but she kisses his cheek and prays aloud for God to bless him as she departs. That night, Jane has a dream in which her mother tells her to flee temptation. She grabs her purse, sneaks down the stairs, and leaves Thornfield.

Chapter 28

Riding in a coach, Jane quickly exhausts her meager money supply and is forced to sleep outdoors. She spends much of the night in prayer, and the following day she begs for food or a job in the nearby town. No one helps her, except for one farmer who is willing to give her a slice of bread. After another day, Jane sees a light shining from across the moors. Following it, she comes to a house. Through the window, Jane sees two young women studying German while their servant knits. From their conversation Jane learns that the servant is named Hannah and that the graceful young women are Diana and Mary. The three women are waiting for someone named St. John (pronounced "Sinjin"). Jane knocks on the door, but Hannah refuses to let her in. Collapsing on the doorstep in anguish and weakness, Jane cries, "I can but die, and I believe in God. Let me try to wait His will in silence." A voice answers, "All men must die, but all are not condemned to meet a lingering and premature doom, such as yours would be if you perished here of want." The voice belongs to "St. John," who brings Jane into the house. He is the brother of Diana and Mary, and the three siblings give Jane food and shelter. They ask her some questions, and she gives them a false name: "Jane Elliott."

Analysis

Feeling . . . clamoured wildly. "Oh, comply!" it said. ". . . soothe him; save him; love him; tell him you love him and will be his. Who in the world cares for you? or who will be injured by what you do?"

Jane endures her most difficult trials in this section of the book: she resolves to leave Rochester although it pains her deeply, and she is forced to sleep outdoors and go hungry on the moors in her flight from Thornfield. However, this section is also where Jane proves to herself her endurance, her strength of principle, and her ability to forge new friendships. As she tells herself before leaving Thornfield, "*I* care for myself. The more solitary, the more friendless, the more unsustained I am, the more I will respect myself." Ultimately this self-interest will make her relationships with others, including her eventual marriage, all the more meaningful and rewarding.

Jane's departure from Thornfield is perhaps the most important decision she makes in the novel. In Rochester she found the love for which she had always yearned, and Thornfield was the first real home she ever knew. In fleeing them, Jane leaves a part of herself behind. But living with Rochester as his mistress would require a self-compromise that Jane is not willing to make. Even before she learns of Bertha's existence, Jane senses that in marrying Rochester she risks cementing herself into a position of inequality. She fears that Rochester would objectify her and that by "marrying above her station" she would come to the relationship already "in debt" to him. Now Jane sees more clearly than ever that a relationship with Rochester would mean the loss of her self-respect, and of her control over her life. Jane cannot bring herself to do what is morally wrong, simply out of weakness of will and emotional neediness.

Despite the happiness and the sense of acceptance that Thornfield and Rochester's love offer, Jane knows that staying would be a type of self-imprisonment. Jane must choose between emotional exile and spiritual and intellectual imprisonment. She knows she must flee while she can.

Throughout the narrative of Jane's trials, the reader not only gains insight into Jane's personal constitution and character, but also into the society in which she lives. When Jane experiences the plight of the poor, the novel presents us with a bleak glimpse of a society in which the needy are shunned out of tightfistedness and distrust.

CHAPTERS 29–32

Summary

Chapter 29

After she is taken in by the Rivers siblings, Jane spends three days recuperating in bed. On the fourth day, she feels well again and follows the smell of baking bread into the kitchen, where she finds Hannah. Jane criticizes Hannah for judging her unfairly when she asked for help, and Hannah apologizes. Hannah tells the story of Mr. Rivers, the siblings' father, who lost most of the family fortune in a bad business deal. In turn, Diana and Mary were forced to work as governesses— they are only at Moors End (or Marsh House) now because their father died three weeks ago. Jane then relates some of her own story and admits that Jane Elliott is not her real name. St. John promises to find her a job.

Chapter 30

Jane befriends Diana and Mary, who admire her drawings and give her books to read. St. John, on the other hand, remains distant and cold, although he is never unkind. After a month, Diana and Mary must return to their posts as governesses. St. John has found a position for Jane, running a charity school for girls in the town of Morton. Jane accepts, but St. John presumes that she will soon leave the school out of restlessness, perhaps because he himself is quite restless. His sisters suspect he will soon leave England for a missionary post overseas. St. John tells his sisters that their Uncle John has died and left them nothing, because all his money went to another, unknown, relative. Jane learns that it was Uncle John who led Mr. Rivers into his disastrous business deal.

Chapter 31

At Morton, the wealthy heiress Rosamond Oliver provides Jane with a cottage in which to live. Jane begins teaching, but to her own regret, she finds the work degrading and disappointing. While on a visit to Jane, St. John reveals that he, too, used to feel that he had made the wrong career choice, until one day he heard God's call. Now he plans to become a missionary. The beautiful Rosamond Oliver then appears, interrupting St. John and Jane's conversation. From their interaction, Jane believes that Rosamond and St. John are in love.

Chapter 32

Jane's students become more familiar and endeared to her, and Jane becomes quite popular among them. At night, though, she has troubling nightmares that involve Rochester. Jane continues to pay attention to the relationship between St. John and Rosamond, who often visits the school when she knows St. John will be there. Rosamond asks Jane to draw her portrait, and as she is working on it one day, St. John pays her a visit. He gives her a new book of poetry (Sir Walter Scott's *Marmion*) and looks at the drawing. She offers to draw him a duplicate, and then boldly declares that he ought to marry Rosamond. St. John admits that he loves her and is tempted by her beauty, but he explains that he refuses to allow worldly affection to interfere with his holy duties. The flirtatious, silly, and shallow Rosamond would make a terrible wife for a missionary. Suddenly, St. John notices something on the edge of Jane's paper and tears off a tiny piece—Jane is not certain why. With a peculiar look on his face, he hurries from the room.

Analysis

Marsh End and Morton are the setting of the novel's fourth phase. Here Jane develops a new sense of belonging, and proves herself capable of finding like-minded companions with whom she is not romantically involved.

The fact that Diana and Mary Rivers are also governesses puts them on an equal footing with Jane. Although Jane left Thornfield convinced that she had made the right decision, she harbored uncertainty as to whether she would ever find a sense of belonging without sacrificing her autonomy. Jane's stay at Marsh End proves to her that she is not doomed to be forever alienated from the world, that a balance between community and autonomy can be achieved. Now, as an integrated member of the Rivers household, Jane realizes that one may give and accept love from others in equal exchange.

When St. John gives Jane Sir Walter Scott's *Marmion,* and Jane-the-narrator comments that this was a new book, it seems as if Brontë is providing a definitive statement about when the events of the novel take place, since *Marmion* was first published in 1808. However, other characters in *Jane Eyre* refer to books published after this date. Blanche Ingram, for instance, refers to Byron's poem *The Corsair* in Chapter 33, but Byron's book wasn't published until 1814. Brontë was obviously not especially concerned with fixing her story in a precise and consistent relation to historical dates, and perhaps she selected the texts mentioned in her novel for other reasons.

CHAPTERS 33–35

Summary

Chapter 33

One snowy night, Jane sits reading *Marmion* when St. John appears at the door. Appearing troubled, he tells Jane the story of an orphan girl who became the governess at Thornfield Hall, then disappeared after nearly marrying Edward Rochester: this runaway governess's name is Jane Eyre. Until this point, Jane has been cautious not to reveal her past and has given the Rivers a false name. Thus although it is clear that St. John suspects her of being the woman about whom he speaks, she does not immediately identify herself to him. He says that he has received a letter from a solicitor named Mr. Briggs intimating that it is extremely important that this Jane Eyre be found. Jane is only interested in whether Mr. Briggs has sent news of Rochester, but St. John says that Rochester's well-being is not at issue: Jane Eyre must be found because her uncle, John Eyre, has died, leaving her the vast fortune of 20,000 pounds.

Jane reveals herself to be Jane Eyre, knowing that St. John has guessed already. She asks him how he knew. He shows her the scrap of paper he tore from her drawing the previous day: it is her signature. She then asks why Mr. Briggs would have sent him a letter about her at all. St. John explains that though he did not realize it before, he is her cousin: her Uncle John was his Uncle John, and his name is St. John Eyre Rivers. Jane is overjoyed to have found a family at long last, and she decides to divide her inheritance between her cousins and herself evenly, so that they each will inherit 5,000 pounds.

Chapter 34

Jane closes her school for Christmas and spends a happy time with her newfound cousins at Moor House. Diana and Mary are delighted with the improvements Jane has made at the school, but St. John seems colder and more distant than ever. He tells Jane that Rosamond is engaged to a rich man named Mr. Granby. One day, he asks Jane to give up her study of German and instead to learn "Hindustani" with him—the language he is learning to prepare for missionary work in India. As time goes by, St. John exerts a greater and greater influence on Jane; his power over her is almost uncanny. This leaves Jane feeling empty, cold, and sad, but she follows his wishes. At last, he asks her to go to India with him to be a missionary—and to be his wife. She agrees to go to India as a missionary but says that she will not be his wife because they are not in love. St. John harshly insists that she marry him, declaring that to refuse his proposal is the same as to deny the Christian faith. He abruptly leaves the room.

Chapter 35

> [B]ut as his wife—at his side always, and always restrained, and always checked—forced to keep the fire of my nature continually low, to compel it to burn inwardly and never utter a cry, though the imprisoned flame consumed vital after vital—this would be unendurable.

During the following week, St. John continues to pressure Jane to marry him. She resists as kindly as she can, but her kindness only makes him insist more bitterly and unyieldingly that she accompany him to India as his wife. Diana tells Jane that she would be a fool to go to India with St. John, who considers her merely a tool to aid his great cause. After dinner, St. John prays for Jane, and she is overcome with awe at his powers of speech and his influence. She almost feels compelled to marry him, but at that moment she hears what she thinks is Rochester's voice, calling her name as if from a great distance. Jane believes that something fateful has occurred, and St. John's spell over her is broken.

Analysis

In these chapters, the foreshadowing of John Eyre's importance in the plot is at last fulfilled, and the household that has initially been for Jane merely a community of social equality is now revealed to be a true family. More importantly, St. John emerges as a crucial figure, providing Jane with a powerful and dangerous alternative to Rochester. All of these experiences prepare the ground for Jane to return to Rochester: having come to know her own strength, having learned that she is no longer alone in the world, having come into her own inheritance, and having received a competing marriage proposal, Jane can now enter into marriage without feeling herself beholden to her husband.

St. John's character emerges forcefully in these chapters. As a potential husband to Jane, he offers a foil to the character of Rochester. Whereas Rochester is passionate and impetuous, St. John is cold, harsh, and clinical. While Jane often finds herself reminding Rochester of the importance of Christian morality, she finds the same morality in St. John overwhelming and threatening.

This leads to St. John's other important function: he provides an interesting comparison to the models of religion embodied in Helen Burns and Mr. Brocklehurst. Unlike the meek and forbearing Helen, St. John is active and even ambitious. He is not hypocritical like Brocklehurst, but he is so rigidly principled and lacking in empathy that his behavior is potentially just as destructive.

Despite Jane's protracted attempt to integrate Christian morality comfortably into her own life and behavior, St. John is a dangerous influence on her, because his forceful personality compels her obedience against her own internal feelings. Jane refuses to marry St. John because she does not love him, but St. John pressures Jane to ignore her feelings and submit to his powerful conception of necessary moral duty. Jane remains true to herself only with great difficulty, and with the help of the preternatural experience of hearing Rochester call out her name over the moors. In declining St. John's proposal Jane escapes yet another threat to her freedom and her sense of self.

Yet the very seriousness with which Jane considers his proposal leads her to an important realization about herself. Part of the reason she fled Thornfield was that she feared becoming a slave to her own passion and sacrificing her principles. By coming so close to marrying St. John, she demonstrates her ability to do the opposite: to sacrifice passion altogether and devote herself wholly to principle. Now Jane knows that returning to Rochester would not signify a weakness on her part. Moreover, she now appreciates more than ever what Rochester offered her. Having found herself on the threshold of a loveless marriage, she understands fully the importance of following not only her mind but also her heart.

CHAPTERS 36–38

Summary

Chapter 36

Jane contemplates her supernatural experience of the previous night, wondering whether it was really Rochester's voice that she heard calling to her and whether Rochester might actually be in trouble. She finds a note from St. John urging her to resist temptation, but nevertheless she boards a coach to Thornfield. She travels to the manor, anxious to see Rochester and reflecting on the ways in which her life has changed in the single year since she left. Once hopeless, alone, and impoverished, Jane now has friends, family, and a fortune. She hurries to the house after her coach arrives and is shocked to find Thornfield a charred ruin. She goes to an inn called the Rochester Arms to learn what has happened. Here, she learns that Bertha Mason set the house ablaze several months earlier. Rochester saved his servants and tried to save his wife, but she flung herself from the roof as the fire raged around her. In the fire, Rochester lost a hand and went blind. He has taken up residence in a house called Ferndean, located deep in the forest, with John and Mary, two elderly servants.

Chapter 37

Jane goes to Ferndean. From a distance, she sees Rochester reach a hand out of the door, testing for rain. His body looks the same, but his face is desperate and disconsolate. Rochester returns inside, and Jane approaches the house. She knocks, and Mary answers the door. Inside, Jane carries a tray to Rochester, who is unable to see her. When he realizes that Jane is in the room with him, he thinks she must be a ghost or spirit speaking to him. When he catches her hand, he takes her in his arms, and she promises never to leave him. The next morning they walk through the woods, and Jane tells Rochester about her experiences the previous year. She has to assure him that she is not in love with St. John. He asks her again to marry him, and she says yes—they are now free from the specter of Bertha Mason. Rochester tells Jane that a few nights earlier, in a moment of desperation, he called out her name and thought he heard her answer. She does not wish to upset him or excite him in his fragile condition, and so she does not tell him about hearing his voice at Moor House.

Chapter 38

Jane and Rochester marry with no witnesses other than the parson and the church clerk. Jane writes to her cousins with the news. St. John never acknowledges what has happened, but Mary and Diana write back with their good wishes. Jane visits Adèle at her school, and finds her unhappy. Remembering her own childhood experience, Jane moves Adèle to a more congenial school, and Adèle grows up to be a very pleasant and mild-mannered young woman.

Jane writes that she is narrating her story after ten years of marriage to Rochester, which she describes as inexpressibly blissful. They live as equals, and she helps him to cope with his blindness. After two years, Rochester begins to regain his vision in one eye, and when their first child—a boy—is born, Rochester is able to see the baby. Jane writes that Diana and Mary have both found husbands and that St. John went to India as he had planned. She notes that in his last letter, St. John claimed to have had a premonition of his own approaching death. She does not believe that she will hear from St. John again, but she does not grieve for him, saying that he has fulfilled his promise and done God's work. She closes her book with a quote from his letter, in which he begs the Lord Jesus to come for him quickly.

Analysis

Jane's melodramatic discovery of the ruined Thornfield and her re-counting of the story of Bertha Mason's mad and fiery death lead to the novel's last, brief stage at Ferndean, during which Jane and Rochester are able to marry at last.

It is possible to question *Jane Eyre*'s proto-feminism on the grounds that Jane only becomes Rochester's full equal (as she claims to be in the novel's epilogue-like last chapter) when he is physically infirm and dependent on her to guide him and read to him—in other words, when he is physically incapable of mastering her. However, it is also possible that Jane now finds herself Rochester's equal not because of the decline Rochester has suffered but because of the autonomy that she has achieved by coming to know herself more fully.

> *No woman was ever nearer to her mate than I am: ever more absolutely bone of his bone, and flesh of his flesh. I know no weariness of my Edward's society: he knows none of mine, any more than we each do of the pulsation of the heart that beats in our separate bosoms; consequently, we are ever together.*

Another problem that troubles some critics is the fact that Jane finds happiness in the novel only through marriage, suggesting that marriage constitutes the only route to contentment for women (after all, the "happy ending" for Diana and Mary, also, is that they find husbands). It could be argued that, in returning to Rochester, Jane sacrifices her long-sought autonomy and independence. Another way of looking at Jane's marriage is that she doesn't sacrifice everything, but enters into a relationship in which giving and taking occur in equal measure. Indeed, in order to marry Rochester Jane has had to reject another marriage, a marriage that would have meant a much more stifling and suppressed life for her. Moreover, in declining to marry St. John, Jane comes to the realization that part of being true to "who she is" means being true to her emotions and passions; part of what makes her *herself* is manifested in her relationships with *others*—in the giving of herself to other human beings. By entering into marriage, Jane does indeed enter into a "bond," but in many ways this "bond" is also the "escape" that Jane has sought all along.

In providing a happy ending for Jane, Brontë seems to suggest that individuals who manage to navigate the pressures and hypocrisies of established social and religious structures can eventually enter into lasting love. A woman who refuses to bend to class and gender prejudices, or to accept domination or oppression, might still find kindred hearts and a sense of spiritual community. Lastly, Brontë seems to suggest a way in which a woman's quest for love and a feeling of belonging need not encroach upon her sense of self—need not restrict her intellectual, spiritual, and emotional independence. Indeed, Brontë suggests that it is only after coming to know oneself and one's own strength that one can enter wholly into a well-rounded and loving relationship with another.

1. I am glad you are no relation of mine. I will never call you aunt again as long as I live. I will never come to visit you when I am grown up; and if any one asks me how I liked you, and how you treated me, I will say the very thought of you makes me sick, and that you treated me with miserable cruelty . . . You think I have no feelings, and that I can do without one bit of love or kindness; but I cannot live so: and you have no pity. I shall remember how you thrust me back . . . into the red-room . . . And that punishment you made me suffer because your wicked boy struck me— knocked me down for nothing. I will tell anybody who asks me questions this exact tale. 'Ere I had finished this reply, my soul began to expand, to exult, with the strangest sense of freedom, of triumph, I ever felt. It seemed as if an invisible bond had burst, and that I had struggled out into unhoped-for liberty. . . .

This quotation, part of Jane's outburst to her aunt just prior to her departure from Gateshead for Lowood School, appears in Chapter 4. In the passage, Jane solidifies her own orphanhood, severing her ties to the little semblance of family that remained to her ("I will never call you aunt again as long as I live," she tells Mrs. Reed). Jane asserts her fiery spirit in her tirade, and she displays a keen sense of justice and a recognition of her need for love. Along with familial liberation, the passage marks Jane's emotional liberation. Jane's imprisonment in the red-room has its psychological counterpart in her emotional suppression, and it is not until she speaks these words to Mrs. Reed that she feels her "soul begin to expand." Lastly, the passage highlights the importance of storytelling as revenge and also as a means of empowerment. Jane declares that she will "tell anybody who asks me questions this exact tale"—via authorship, Jane asserts her authority over and against her tyrannical aunt.

2. Feeling . . . clamoured wildly. "Oh, comply!" it said. ". . . soothe him; save him; love him; tell him you love him and will be his. Who in the world cares for *you*? or who will be injured by what you do?" Still indomitable was the reply: "*I* care for myself. The more solitary, the more friendless, the more unsustained I am, the more I will respect myself. I will keep the law given by God; sanctioned by man. I will hold to the principles received by me when I was sane, and not mad—as I am now. Laws and principles are not for the times when there is no temptation . . . They have a worth—so I have always believed; and if I cannot believe it now, it is because I am insane—quite insane: with my veins running fire, and my heart beating faster than I can count its throbs."

In this quotation, near the end of Chapter 27, Jane asserts her strong sense of moral integrity over and against her intense immediate feelings. Rochester has been trying to convince her to stay with him despite the fact that he is still legally married to Bertha Mason. His argument almost persuades Jane: Rochester is the first person who has ever truly loved her. Yet she knows that staying with him would mean compromising herself, because she would be Rochester's mistress rather than his wife. Not only would she lose her self-respect, she would probably lose Rochester's, too, in the end. Thus Jane asserts her worth and her ability to love herself regardless of how others treat her.

The passage also sheds light upon Jane's understanding of religion. She sees God as the giver of the laws by which she must live. When she can no longer trust herself to exercise good judgment, she looks to these principles as an objective point of reference.

Jane's allusions to her "madness" and "insanity" bring out an interesting parallel between Jane and Bertha Mason. It is possible to see Bertha as a double for Jane, who embodies what Jane feels within—especially since the externalization of interior sentiment is a trait common to the Gothic novel.

The description of Jane's blood running like "fire" constitutes one of many points in the book in which Jane is associated with flames.

3. "Shall I?" I said briefly; and I looked at his features, beautiful in their harmony, but strangely formidable in their still sever-

ity; at his brow, commanding, but not open; at his eyes, bright and deep and searching, but never soft; at his tall imposing figure; and fancied myself in idea *his wife*. Oh! it would never do! As his curate, his comrade, all would be right: I would cross oceans with him in that capacity; toil under Eastern suns, in Asian deserts with him in that office; admire and emulate his courage and devotion and vigour: accommodate quietly to his masterhood; smile undisturbed at his ineradicable ambition. . . . I should suffer often, no doubt, attached to him only in this capacity: my body would be under a rather stringent yoke, but my heart and mind would be free. I should still have my unblighted self to turn to: my natural unenslaved feelings with which to communicate in moments of loneliness. There would be recesses in my mind which would be only mine, to which he never came; and sentiments growing there, fresh and sheltered, which his austerity could never blight, nor his measured warrior-march trample down: but as his wife—at his side always, and always restrained, and always checked—forced to keep the fire of my nature continually low, to compel it to burn inwardly and never utter a cry, though the imprisoned flame consumed vital after vital—*this* would be unendurable.

This passage occurs in Chapter 34. St. John Rivers has just asked Jane to join him as his wife on his missionary trip to India. Jane dramatizes the interior conflict involved in making her decision. In many ways, the proposal tempts her. It is an opportunity to perform good works and to be more than a governess, schoolteacher, or housewife—the roles traditionally open to women. Jane's teaching jobs at Lowood, Thornfield, and Morton have all made her feel trapped, and she would not mind enduring hardships for a cause in which she truly believes. Yet, St. John's principles—"ambition," "austerity," and arrogance—are not those that Jane upholds.

Misguided religion threatens to oppress Jane throughout the book, and St. John merely embodies one form of it. He also embodies masculine dominance, another force that threatens Jane like a "stringent yoke" over the course of the novel. Thus she describes St. John's "warrior-march" and notes his assertion of his "masterhood." Jane must escape such control in order to

remain true to herself, for she realizes that her conventional manner of deal-
ing with oppression—by retreating into herself, into the recesses of her
imagination, into conversation with herself—cannot constitute a way of life.
In her rejection of Rochester, Jane privileged principle over feeling; she is
now aware of the negative effects such emotional repression can have. Feeling, too, must play a role in one's life: a balance must be struck.

4. I could not help it; the restlessness was in my nature; it agi-
   tated me to pain sometimes. Then my sole relief was to walk
   along the corridor of the third story, backwards and for-
   wards, safe in the silence and solitude of the spot, and allow
   my mind's eye to dwell on whatever bright visions rose before
   it—and, certainly, they were many and glowing; to let my
   heart be heaved by the exultant movement . . . and, best of all,
   to open my inward ear to a tale that was never ended—a tale
   my imagination created, and narrated continuously; quick-
   ened with all of incident, life, fire, feeling, that I desired and
   had not in my actual existence. It is in vain to say human beings ought to be satisfied with tranquility: they must have action; and they will make it if they cannot find it. Millions are
   condemned to a stiller doom than mine, and millions are in
   silent revolt against their lot. Nobody knows how many rebellions besides political rebellions ferment in the masses of
   life which people earth. Women are supposed to be very calm
   generally: but women feel just as men feel; they need exercise
   for their faculties, and a field for their efforts as much as their
   brothers do; they suffer from too rigid a restraint, too absolute a stagnation, precisely as men would suffer; and it is
   narrow-minded in their more privileged fellow-creatures to
   say that they ought to confine themselves to making pud-
   dings and knitting stockings, to playing on the piano and
   embroidering bags. It is thoughtless to condemn them, or
   laugh at them, if they seek to do more or learn more than
   custom has pronounced necessary for their sex.

This passage appears in Chapter 12, in the midst of Jane's description of
her first few weeks at Thornfield. The diction highlights Jane's feelings of

imprisonment (she paces the corridors like a creature caged), and her longings for freedom and equality. Jane's words are also relevant to Brontë's own experience as a writer, and to the general condition of Victorian women.

The images of restlessness and pacing, of feeling "stagnation" and "too rigid a restraint," are examples of the book's central theme of imprisonment. In addition to instances of physical imprisonment, Jane must also escape the fetters of misguided religion (represented by Brocklehurst), of passion without principle (represented at first by Rochester), and of principle without passion (represented by St. John Rivers)—not to mention those of society.

Brocklehurst, Rochester, and St. John may also threaten Jane with the fetters of patriarchy, which is the specific force Jane resists in this passage. Jane extends her feeling of entrapment to her fellow women, and these sentences constitute Brontë's feminist manifesto. As she describes the "doom" to which "millions in silent revolt against their lot" "are condemned," Brontë criticizes what she believed to be stifling Victorian conceptions of proper gender roles. The passage explicitly states that the Victorian wife suffers from being metaphorically "locked up." Bertha Mason, who is eventually rendered nearly inhuman when her neglected, suppressed feelings turn to madness and fury, may be viewed as a symbol of the imprisoned female's condition.

The passage suggests that Brontë's writing may have been her means of coping with such rage. Jane describes her retreat into her own mind, to find freedom in her imagination. While Brontë's greatest triumphs were the result of such self-retreat, her heroine's achievement is the balance she strikes between her need for autonomy and her desire to be an active member of society.

5. I have now been married ten years. I know what it is to live entirely for and with what I love best on earth. I hold myself supremely blest—blest beyond what language can express; because I am my husband's life as fully as he is mine. No woman was ever nearer to her mate than I am: ever more absolutely bone of his bone, and flesh of his flesh. I know no weariness of my Edward's society: he knows none of mine, any more than we each do of the pulsation of the heart that beats in our separate bosoms; consequently, we are ever to-

gether. To be together is for us to be at once as free as in solitude, as gay as in company. We talk, I believe, all day long: to talk to each other is but a more animated and an audible thinking. All my confidence is bestowed on him, all his confidence is devoted to me; we are precisely suited in character—perfect concord is the result.

This, one of the final passages of *Jane Eyre,* summarizes the novel's "happy ending." Its implications have generated much debate over the way Brontë chose to conclude her book. Some critics view Jane as having sacrificed her autonomy—no longer her own person, she and Rochester have merged, sharing one heart, each possessing the "bone" and "flesh" of the other.

One might also argue that Jane relinquishes her powers of thought and expression—two characteristics that have defined her for most of the novel. Suddenly, the otherwise imaginative Jane equates her "thinking" to her conversations with Rochester—she even finds the conversations "more animated." Similarly, although ten years have elapsed since the wedding, the otherwise eloquent Jane suddenly claims that she is unable to find any "language" to "express" her experiences during this period.

Other critics interpret this passage in a more positive manner. It can be read as Jane's affirmation of the equality between her and Rochester, as testimony that she has not "given up" anything. The passage is followed in the novel by a report on St. John Rivers. Jane writes: "his is the spirit of the warrior Greatheart . . . his is the ambition of the high master-spirit. . . ." (Greatheart serves as guide to the pilgrims in Bunyan's *Pilgrim's Progress.*) Emphasizing St. John's desires for "mastery" and his "warrior" characteristics, Jane describes a controlling patriarch. While Rochester may have been such a figure at the beginning of the novel, his character has changed by its conclusion. He has lost his house, his hand, and his eyesight to a fire, and the revelation of his youthful debaucheries has shown him to be Jane's moral inferior. Rochester can no longer presume to be Jane's "master" in any sense. Moreover, Jane has come to Rochester this second time in economic independence and by free choice; at Moor House she found a network of love and support, and she does not depend solely on Rochester for emotional nurturance. Optimistic critics point to Jane's description of St. John as her reminder that the marriage she rejected would have offered her a much more stifling life. By entering into marriage, Jane does enter into a sort of "bond"; yet in many ways this "bond" is the "escape" that she has sought all along. Perhaps Brontë meant Jane's closing words to celebrate her attainment of freedom; it is also possible that Brontë meant us to bemoan the tragic paradox of Jane's situation.

FULL TITLE
Jane Eyre

AUTHOR
Charlotte Brontë (originally published under the male pseudonym Currer Bell)

TYPE OF WORK
Novel

GENRE
A hybrid of three genres: the Gothic novel (utilizes the mysterious, the supernatural, the horrific, the romantic); the romance novel (emphasizes love and passion, represents the notion of lovers destined for each other); and the *Bildungsroman* (narrates the story of a character's internal development as he or she undergoes a succession of encounters with the external world)

LANGUAGE
English

TIME AND PLACE WRITTEN
1847 London

DATE OF FIRST PUBLICATION
1847

PUBLISHER
Smith, Elder, and Co., Cornhill

NARRATOR
Jane Eyre

CLIMAX
The novel's climax comes after Jane receives her second marriage proposal of the novel—this time from St. John Rivers, who asks Jane to accompany him to India as his wife and fellow missionary. Jane considers the proposal, even though she knows that marrying St. John would mean the death of her emotional life. She is on the

verge of accepting when she hears Rochester's voice supernaturally calling her name from across the heath and knows that she must return to him. She can retain her dignity in doing so because she has proven to herself that she is not a slave to passion.

PROTAGONIST

Jane Eyre

ANTAGONIST

Jane meets with a series of forces that threaten her liberty, integrity, and happiness. Characters embodying these forces are: Aunt Reed, Mr. Brocklehurst, Bertha Mason, Mr. Rochester (in that he urges Jane to ignore her conscience and surrender to passion), and St. John Rivers (in his urging of the opposite extreme). The three men also represent the notion of an oppressive patriarchy. Blanche Ingram, who initially stands in the way of Jane's relations with Rochester, also embodies the notion of a rigid class system—another force keeping Jane from fulfilling her hopes.

SETTING (TIME)

Early decades of the 19th century.

SETTING (PLACE)

The novel is structured around five separate locations, all supposedly in northern England: the Reed family's home at Gateshead, the wretched Lowood School, Rochester's manor house Thornfield, the Rivers family's home at Moor House, and Rochester's rural retreat at Ferndean.

POINT OF VIEW

All of the events are told from Jane's point of view. Sometimes she narrates the events as she experienced them at the time, while at other times she focuses on her retrospective understanding of the events.

FALLING ACTION

After Jane hears Rochester's call to her from across the heath, she returns to Thornfield and finds it burned to the ground. She learns that Bertha Mason set the fire and died in the flames; Rochester is now living at his home in Ferndean. Jane goes to him there, rebuilds her relationship with the somewhat humbled Rochester, and marries him. She claims to enjoy perfect equality in her marriage.

TENSE

Past-tense; Jane Eyre tells her story ten years after the last event in the novel, her arrival at Ferndean.

FORESHADOWING

The novel's main instances of foreshadowing focus on Jane's eventual inheritance (Chapter 33) from her uncle John Eyre. In Chapter 3, Jane tells Mr. Lloyd that her aunt has told her of some "poor, low relations called Eyre," but she knows nothing more about them. Jane first receives hints of her uncle's existence in Chapter 10 when Bessie visits her at Lowood and mentions that her father's brother appeared at Gateshead seven years ago, looking for Jane. He did not have the time to come to Lowood, she explains, and he subsequently went away to Madeira (a Portuguese island west of Morocco) in search of wealth. Foreshadowing again enters into the novel in Chapter 21, when, returning to Gateshead to see her dying Aunt Reed for the last time, Jane learns that her uncle had written to her aunt three years earlier, reporting that he had been successful in Madeira and expressing his desire to adopt Jane and make her his heir; her aunt had deliberately ignored the letter out of spite. Another powerful instance of foreshadowing is the chestnut tree under which Rochester proposes to Jane. Before they leave, Jane mentions that it "writhed and groaned," and that night, it splits in two, forecasting complications for Jane and Rochester's relationship (Chapter 23).

TONE

Jane Eyre's tone is both Gothic and romantic, often conjuring an atmosphere of mystery, secrecy, or even horror. Despite these Gothic elements, Jane's personality is friendly and the tone is also affectionate and confessional. Her unflagging spirit and opinionated nature further infuse the book with high energy and add a philosophical and political flavor.

THEMES

Love versus autonomy; religion; social class; gender relations

MOTIFS

Fire and ice; substitute mothers

SYMBOLS

Bertha Mason; the red-room

STUDY QUESTIONS

1. *In what ways is* Jane Eyre *influenced by the tradition of the Gothic novel? What do the Gothic elements contribute to the novel?*

The Gothic tradition utilizes elements such as supernatural encounters, remote locations, complicated family histories, ancient manor houses, dark secrets, and mysteries to create an atmosphere of suspense and terror, and the plot of *Jane Eyre* includes most of these elements. Lowood, Moor House, and Thornfield are all remote locations, and Thornfield, like Gateshead, is also an ancient manor house. Both Rochester and Jane possess complicated family histories—Rochester's hidden wife, Bertha, is the dark secret at the novel's core. The exposure of Bertha is one of the most important moments in the novel, and the mystery surrounding her is the main source of the novel's suspense.

Other Gothic occurrences include: Jane's encounter with the ghost of her late Uncle Reed in the red-room; the moment of supernatural communication between Jane and Rochester when she hears his voice calling her across the misty heath from miles and miles away; and Jane's mistaking Rochester's dog, Pilot, for a "Gytrash," a spirit of North England that manifests itself as a horse or dog.

Although Brontë's use of Gothic elements heightens her reader's interest and adds to the emotional and philosophical tensions of the book, most of the seemingly supernatural occurrences are actually explained as the story progresses. It seems that many of the Gothic elements serve to anticipate and elevate the importance of the plot's turning points.

2. *What do the names mean in* Jane Eyre? *Some names to consider include: Jane Eyre, Gateshead, Lowood, Thornfield, Reed, Rivers, Miss Temple, and Ferndean.*

Of course, there are many possible ways to address this question. The following answer includes only a few of the ways the names in *Jane Eyre* can be interpreted.

The name "Jane Eyre" elicits many associations. The contrast between Jane's first name—with its traditional association with "plainness"—and the names of the novel's well-born women (Blanche, Eliza, Georgiana, Diana, Rosamond) highlights Jane's lack of status, but it also emphasizes her lack of pretense. Jane's last name has many possible interpretations, none of which mutually excludes the other. "Eyre" is an archaic spelling for "air," and throughout the book, Jane is linked to the spiritual or ethereal as she drifts, windlike, from one location to the next. In French, "aire" refers to a bird's nesting place, among other things. Jane is compared to a bird repeatedly throughout the novel, and she often uses her imagination as a "nesting-place" of sorts, a private realm where she can feel secure. In medieval times, "eyre" also signified circuit-traveling judges. Perhaps Jane's name is meant to bring attention to her role as a careful evaluator of all that she sees, and to the importance that she attaches to justice. "Eyre" also sounds like "heir," and its other homophone—"err"—could certainly be interpreted to be meaningful, especially to feminist and religious critics who take issue with Jane's actions!

Place names also seem to be symbolic. Jane's story begins at "Gateshead." From there, she moves to the bosky darkness and spiritual abyss of "Lowood." At Thornfield, she must fight her way through the stings of many emotional and psychological thorns (or, as many critics argue, wear "a crown of thorns" like Jesus Christ). Jane first tastes true freedom of movement in the open spaces surrounding Moor House, while Ferndean is the home where her love can grow fertile. Thus in Chapter 37 Rochester says to Jane, "I am no better than the old lightning-struck chestnut-tree in Thornfield orchard . . . And what right would that ruin have to bid a budding woodbine cover its decay with freshness?" Jane replies, "You are no ruin, sir—no lightning-struck tree: you are green and vigorous. Plants will grow about your roots, whether you ask them or not, because they take delight in your bountiful shadow; and as they grow they will lean towards you, and wind round you, because your strength offers them so safe a prop."

SUGGESTED ESSAY TOPICS

1. Discuss Jane as a narrator and as a character. What sort of voice does she have? How does she represent her own actions? Does she seem to be a trustworthy storyteller, or does Brontë require us to read between the lines of her narrative? In light of the fact that people who treat Jane cruelly (John Reed, Mrs. Reed, Mr. Brocklehurst) all seem to come to unhappy endings, what role does Jane play as the novel's moral center?

2. In what ways might *Jane Eyre* be considered a feminist novel? What points does the novel make about the treatment and position of women in Victorian society? With particular attention to the book's treatment of marriage, is there any way in which it might be considered anti-feminist?

3. What role does Jane's ambiguous social position play in determining the conflict of her story? What larger points, if any, does the novel make about social class? Does the book criticize or reinforce existing Victorian social prejudices? Consider the treatment of Jane as a governess, but also of the other servants in the book, along with Jane's attitude toward her impoverished students at Morton.

4. Compare and contrast some of the characters who serve as foils throughout *Jane Eyre*: Blanche to Jane, St. John to Rochester, and, perhaps, Bertha to Jane. Also think about the points of comparison between the Reed and Rivers families. How do these contrasts aid the development of the book's themes?

QUIZ

1. What are the names of the servants who care for Rochester at Ferndean?
    A. John and Clara
    B. Reginald and Mrs. Fairfax
    C. Mrs. Fairfax and Grace Poole
    D. John and Mary

2. Which character is in love with Rosamond?
    A. St. John
    B. Rochester
    C. John Reed
    D. Mr. Mason

3. Who sets the fire in Rochester's bedroom?
    A. Jane
    B. Bertha
    C. Mrs. Fairfax
    D. Grace Poole

4. What has just happened to Mr. Mason the first time we encounter him?
    A. He has fallen from the roof
    B. He has been injured
    C. He has been poisoned
    D. He has fallen in love

5. Which character is based on the Reverend Carus Wilson, a figure from Charlotte Brontë's childhood?
    A. St. John Rivers
    B. Rochester
    C. Mr. Brocklehurst
    D. Mr. Lloyd

6. *Who writes to St. John regarding Jane's inheritance from John Eyre?*
   A. Mr. Briggs
   B. Mr. Mason
   C. Mr. Brocklehurst
   D. Mrs. Reed

7. *How does John Reed apparently die?*
   A. He falls from the roof of Thornfield
   B. He is killed in a fire
   C. He has a stroke
   D. He commits suicide

8. *Where did Rochester marry Bertha Mason?*
   A. Jamaica
   B. Madeira
   C. St. Kitts
   D. Bermuda

9. *Who first suggests that Jane be sent away to school?*
   A. Mrs. Reed
   B. Mr. Brocklehurst
   C. Mr. Lloyd
   D. John Reed

10. *What is the nationality of Jane's pupil at Thornfield?*
    A. Spanish
    B. German
    C. Jamaican
    D. French

11. *What does Rochester lose in the fire at Thornfield?*
    A. His hand and his eyesight
    B. His eyesight and his fortune
    C. His eyesight and his dog
    D. His fortune and his fiancée

12. Which teacher is kind to Jane at Lowood?
    A. Mrs. Scatcherd
    B. Miss Temple
    C. Mr. Brocklehurst
    D. Miss Ames

13. What does the kind teacher give Jane and Helen to eat?
    A. Bundt cake
    B. Strawberries
    C. Cookies
    D. Seed cake

14. How does Jane earn a living after leaving Thornfield?
    A. She paints
    B. She writes and sells short stories
    C. She becomes a governess at a different manor house
    D. St. John Rivers finds her a teaching job in the town of Morton

15. With whom does Jane believe Rochester is in love for most of her time at Thornfield?
    A. Herself
    B. Blanche Ingram
    C. Georgianna Reed
    D. Celine Varens

16. What does Jane do with the inheritance she receives from her uncle John Eyre?
    A. She divides it equally among her cousins the Rivers
    B. She starts a school in the town of Morton
    C. She sends it to Gateshead to comfort the Reeds for the death of their mother
    D. She buys ball gowns and jewelry for herself

17. *What is the nature of Jane's first encounter with Rochester?*
  A. Rochester comes to Lowood to enroll Adèle there, but Jane warns him about the coldness and isolation at Lowood and recommends that he hire her as Adèle's live-in governess instead
  B. After having been abroad for some time, Rochester returns to Thornfield and sends for Jane to come to him in his library
  C. Jane and Rochester were long lost childhood sweethearts
  D. Jane helps a stranger whose horse has slipped on some ice; she discovers later that the man was Rochester

18. *What does Mr. Brocklehurst do to one of Jane's classmates to rid her of her "vanity"?*
  A. He makes her wear a dunce cap
  B. He has her naturally curly hair cut short so as to make it lie straight
  C. He forces her to write, "I am a very silly girl" on the chalkboard 100 times
  D. He puts a curtain over her bedroom mirror

19. *How does Jane's Aunt Reed punish her for fighting with her bullying cousin John?*
  A. She makes her sleep outside in the cold
  B. She makes her eat only burnt porridge
  C. She makes her shine John's shoes for a week
  D. She locks her in the red-room

20. *To which destination does St. John Rivers want Jane to accompany him as his wife and fellow missionary?*
  A. India
  B. China
  C. The Congo
  D. Ireland

21. *What is the name of the Riverses' servant?*
  A. Alice
  B. Bertha
  C. Hannah
  D. Persephone

22. *What does Jane do immediately after finishing her studies at Lowood?*
   A. She answers an advertisement for a governess at Thornfield
   B. She becomes a teacher there
   C. She burns down the building
   D. She is forced to wander penniless and starving across the moors

23. *Who wears the disguise of a gypsy woman?*
   A. Blanche Ingram
   B. Rochester
   C. Lady Ingram
   D. Lady Bartholomew

24. *What happens within the first ten years of Jane and Rochester's marriage?*
   A. A daughter is born
   B. A son is born
   C. A star is born
   D. None of the above

25. *What is the subject of the book Jane is reading at the beginning of the novel?*
   A. Fish
   B. British royalty
   C. Fairies and knights
   D. Birds

SUGGESTIONS FOR FURTHER READING

Barker, Juliet R. V. *The Brontës*. New York: St. Martin's Press, 1995.

Berg, Maggie. *Jane Eyre: Portrait of a Life*. Boston: Twayne Publishers, 1987.

Bloom, Harold, ed. *Charlotte Brontë's Jane Eyre*. New York: Chelsea House Publishers, 1987.

Brontë, Charlotte. *Jane Eyre: An Authoritative Text, Backgrounds, Criticism*. Richard J. Dunn, ed. New York: W.W. Norton & Co., 1971.

Fraser, Rebecca. *The Brontës: Charlotte Brontë and her Family*. New York: Crown Publishers, 1988.

Gates, Barbara Timm, ed. *Critical Essays on Charlotte Brontë*. Boston: G.K. Hall & Co., 1990.

Gilbert, Sandra M. and Susan Gubar, eds. *The Madwoman in the Attic: The Woman Writer and the Nineteenth-Century Imagination*. New Haven: Yale University Press, 1979.

Gregor, Ian, ed. *The Brontës*. Englewood Cliffs, New Jersey: Prentice Hall, 1970.

Rhys, Jean. *Wide Sargasso Sea*. New York: W.W. Norton & Co., 1999.

Vicinus, Martha, ed. *Suffer and Be Still: Women in the Victorian Age*. Bloomington: Indiana University Press, 1972.

Winnifrith, Tom. *The Brontës and their Background: Romance and Reality*. Houndmills, Basingstoke, Hampshire: Macmillan, 1988.